The Uncensored Bible

The Uncensored Bible

The Bawdy and Naughty Bits of the Good Book

John Kaltner, Steven L. McKenzie,
and Joel Kilpatrick

HarperOne
An Imprint of HarperCollins*Publishers*

THE UNCENSORED BIBLE: *The Bawdy and Naughty Bits of the Good Book*. Copyright © 2008 by John Kaltner, Steven L. McKenzie, and Joel Kilpatrick. All rights reserved. Printed in the United States of America. No part of this book may be used or reproduced in any manner whatsoever without written permission except in the case of brief quotations embodied in critical articles and reviews. For information address HarperCollins Publishers, 10 East 53rd Street, New York, NY 10022.

HarperCollins books may be purchased for educational, business, or sales promotional use. For information please write: Special Markets Department, HarperCollins Publishers, 10 East 53rd Street, New York, NY 10022.

HarperCollins Web site: http://www.harpercollins.com

HarperCollins®, ■ ®, and HarperOne™ are trademarks of HarperCollins Publishers.

FIRST EDITION

Library of Congress Cataloging-in-Publication Data is available upon request.

ISBN 978–0–06–123884–0

08 09 10 11 12   RRD (H)   10 9 8 7 6 5 4 3 2 1

To C.E.W.

*Books are like people—
sometimes you just can't believe
what's in them.*

Contents

Acknowledgments

Writing a book shouldn't be this much fun. From start to finish we've had a rollicking time, and along the way we've benefited from the feedback of friends and loved ones. First, we'd like to thank the "Eves" in our lives, Debra Bartelli and Aimee McCarley, for their suggestions and encouragement. They, better than anyone, know what it's like to put up with a middle-aged Bible scholar who's become obsessed with his latest project.

Several people associated with Rhodes College, in Memphis, Tennessee, read drafts of some of the chapters and provided helpful comments on our work. A special thanks to Bob Johnson, Mike LaRosa, Spence and Becky Wilson, and Karen Winterton.

We tried out some of the material in this book with a group of adult students in Rhodes's Meeman Center for Continuing Education. "The Bawdy Bible" turned out to be one of those special experiences that teachers live for and convinced us that we were on the right track with the book. The class, now a tight circle of friends, consisted of Phyllis and Tandy Brannon, Gloria Gang, Marshall Gordon, Jimmy Humphreys, Jim Johnson, Martha Kelly, Ed Murphey, Martha Robbins, and Norm Shapiro.

Steve has also been able to sneak sections of "The Bawdy Bible" into his course offerings for Rhodes students over the past two years. As is typical of our students, they taught him more than he taught them, with observations about these ancient texts and their modern interpreters that were innovative and insightful.

Our agent, Gary Heidt, is one of those rare individuals who believe there's a place in the world for a book on weird Bible stories and interpretations. He helped us give shape to our original concept and found the perfect publisher for the book. HarperOne was our "dream" choice from the beginning, and we're thrilled that Gary was able to land the book with them. It has been a great pleasure to work with Kris Ashley of HarperOne. She is an outstanding editor, and we very much appreciate her guidance and enthusiasm.

Finally, we are deeply grateful to our co-author Joel Kilpatrick, who has helped us turn unusual but still dry Bible scholarship into entertaining reading. We thought we were funny guys until we read our manuscript after Joel had spun it. We laughed out loud at least once on nearly every page, but we recognize that everyone may not share our perverted sense of humor. We take full responsibility for the discussions and judgments about Bible scholarship in this book. But Joel is to blame for any jokes that fall flat.

—John Kaltner
Steve McKenzie

Introduction

―◦∾◦―

"In the Beginning";
or,
How John and Steve Got the Idea
for Writing This Book

There we were, enjoying the cool air and a couple of adult beverages in the middle of summer in Nova Scotia. We had escaped the sweltering heat of Memphis, Tennessee, where we live and teach, to attend a conference of Bible scholars. But we weren't exactly at the conference at the moment—we were in a nearby bar playing hooky and relaxing. Who could blame us? We had endured dust-dry seminars with names like "Observations on the Hebrew Narrative of Genesis 2:4–4:1" and worse. Even highly trained ancient language scholars like us can take only so much before heading for the nearest watering hole.

But instead of discussing the fine weather, sports, or the sad demise of the Canadian stubby, we found ourselves talking about the presentation we'd just heard. To our surprise, it had not been the tedious analysis of the Garden of Eden story we'd expected, as would have been typical fare for such a gathering. Rather, it was one of the most unusual, provocative, and—yes—sexy presentations we had ever heard at a Bible conference.

The presenter was a guy named Ziony Zevit (great name, huh?), who is a well-known and respected scholar at the American Jewish University (formerly the University of Judaism in Los Angeles, California). In his analysis of the Adam and Eve story, Zevit suggested that the commonly held belief that Genesis describes Eve's creation from Adam's rib might be wrong. It is more likely, he argued, that the text refers to Eve's creation from another bone, the *baculum*. That probably doesn't sound shocking to you now, but just wait until you read chapter 1 and learn what the *baculum* is. We were blown away by Zevit's proposal. His idea was clever, creative, and off-color enough to make for interesting bar talk. It had the added benefit of being highly plausible.

Zevit had actually published his suggestive theory in an obscure medical journal, but it hadn't exactly gotten him on Letterman. As we enjoyed our margaritas and mojitos, we began to shoot the bull about how many other provocative and impolite interpretations of Bible passages get published only to circulate briefly in the rarefied air of Bible scholarship before dropping from sight. Turns out, quite a few. That evening, perhaps intoxicated by the Canadian air and the bartender's liberal pouring methods, we decided to compile a collection of weird and bawdy Bible stories and interpretations for wider circulation—a sort of Baedeker to gross, risqué, and deliciously disgusting Bible scholarship for the common man and woman.

We were not just interested in looking at odd interpretations of the Bible. There are plenty of those out there. Our focus was on interpretations that are unusual but viable and that have been offered by not just anybody but by people who are bona-fide Bible scholars. So we rigorously applied what we call the "Zevit Standard" to the long list of potentials that we initially compiled. The Zevit Standard consists of four criteria:

1. The proposed interpretation has to be innovative and un-usual. By "unusual" we mean outrageous, juicy, and ribald—the stranger the better.

2. It has to offer a new take on a familiar Bible passage. Most of the stories and people we cover in this book will be familiar to you.

3. It has to be plausible—well argued and worth serious con-sideration.

4. It has to be authored by someone trained in biblical studies. Usually this means a person with a PhD in biblical studies who makes a living teaching the Bible in a college, university, or seminary. The few exceptions in this book are people who are self-trained, have published books on the Bible, and have gained a certain expertise.

The Zevit Standard still left us plenty of interpretations to choose from, and we whittled those down to a manageable two dozen or so of our favorites—some of which will surely surprise you as much as they did us.

No Bible Bashing, Please

We want to make it clear that we're not trying to make fun of the Bible. We love the Bible. In fact, part of what we hope to accom-plish with this book is to help people appreciate the Bible more. We agree that the Bible should be read with reverence. But part of the Bible's richness stems from the fact that it comes out of and reflects real life in all of its complex beauty and weirdness. The Bible deals with the sublime and the very mundane—important issues like the meaning of life and the majesty of God, but also such run-of-the-mill matters as breeding animals and managing your own sex life. Since the Bible comes from a different time and culture, modern readers may tend to miss or misunderstand some of those earthy texts, especially if our focus is on the divine and holy. We hope this book increases readers' appreciation for the richness and diversity of the Bible's contents.

We also aren't out to ridicule Bible scholarship. Heck, we're Bible scholars ourselves. We have doctoral degrees from universities that, at least until this book was published, were respected institutions of higher learning. We also teach Bible in a liberal arts college, although it's our wives who really earn a living for us. We love what we do. And we love our fellow Bible geeks, er . . . scholars.

Of course, just because a person is a scholar doesn't mean his or her interpretations are right. And just because an interpretation is new doesn't mean it's correct. Bible scholars sometimes float ideas that are lead balloons. We've included a few examples of these in this book because they're so odd and preposterous that we couldn't resist taking a swipe at them. But for the most part, each of the proposals we discuss has some merit and needs to be carefully evaluated before it gets a thumbs-up or a thumbs-down.

So how do we decide if an interpretation is right or not? Bible scholarship isn't math or rocket science, so the rules are less clear, but there are still plenty of ways to get at the truth by weighing the linguistic evidence, looking at archaeological findings, and using plain old common sense. Each case has to be evaluated in its own unique way, and when you make it through to the end of the book, you should have a pretty good sense of how Bible scholars earn their living.

It has been said that no other book has been read more throughout history than the Bible, and that no other book has been more misunderstood or misinterpreted. We agree with that sentiment, and with this book we wish to bring out from the shadows one of the least understood dimensions of the text—the bawdy side of the Bible, if you will. This book presents the Bible in its wide range of experiences, from the profound and beautiful to the weird, bizarre, and downright shocking. It shines the bright light of scholarship on some of the sexiest and strangest parts of the Bible. Beyond that, we have no other objectives or hidden agenda. Well, except to snare a guest spot on *The Daily Show*. . . . So hold your nose, tighten your gut, and get your "Oh, dear" expressions good and ready—'cause here we go.

Which "Bone" Was Eve Made From?

As famous as some Hollywood couples are, nobody can approach the fame of Adam and Eve, Earth's original celebrity couple. Almost *everybody* knows about Adam and Eve, even if they know nothing else about the Bible.

But a lot of people, Bible readers included, don't know that Eve's origins may have been quite different from what many of us learned in Sunday school. In fact, the true explanation for where Eve came from may be as scandalous as a tabloid headline ("Eve's Shocking Past!"). We'll get to that, but first, let's have a look at the traditional story most people know.

The biblical account of creation is told in the second chapter of the Book of Genesis, which describes how God made the earth and heavens and then planted an idyllic, tree-filled nature park—the Garden of Eden. This Garden apparently was the "it" place on planet Earth. Adam and Eve would hang out there, as would an assortment of amazing creatures, including a talking snake. God would even drop by in the evenings to liven up the party. In fact, Adam and Eve had a pretty good deal overall. They owned an entire planet (and paid no property taxes on it). The only requirements God placed on them were to (1) have sex and (2) hold down fairly easy gardening and animal husbandry jobs. They blew it, of course, but that's another story.

Let's go back a little further, to Adam's origins. God created the Garden of Eden, then formed the first man, Adam, from the ground, as a potter would form a vessel out of clay, and placed him in the Garden to take care of it. But at some point God appears to have decided that having one human being around, and nobody with whom that human could share his silly little observations, was a recipe for loneliness and depression. "It is not good for the man to be alone," God said, according to Genesis, so God took some mud, as he had done with Adam, and created other dirt creatures to be the man's companions. But these newbies were animals, not humans. God organized them into a pet parade, brought them before Adam, and invited him to name them. But as entertaining as this exotic animal collection no doubt was, none of the creatures suited Adam's need for a soul mate, a colleague, or even a drinking buddy. He was stuck with his loneliness problem, and no MySpace, eHarmony, or Prozac to turn to. He had a dog (and a lion, and a giraffe . . .), but he still didn't have a best friend.

So God administered the world's first anesthesia and put Adam into a deep sleep so God could perform surgery. While Adam was under, God removed one of his ribs, as the traditional story goes. From that rib, God then made the first woman, Eve, and brought her to the man. Adam's response upon seeing her, according to the Bible, was, "Bone of my bones and flesh of my flesh," which can also be translated from the Hebrew as, "Va-va-va-voom!" He called her "Wo-*man*," a play on words, because she was taken from *man* and was a lot like him except in some key, very attractive regards. The story adds a postscript, explaining that this is the reason why a man leaves his parents and is united with his wife so that they become one flesh. Keep that postscript and that word "flesh" in mind. They will help us to see what this passage really might be saying.

Problems with the Traditional Interpretation

The traditional version of the story is accurate to the text except for one important detail. Though for centuries the term "Adam's rib" has been used in sermons, commentaries, and film titles (see "Spencer Tracy and Katharine Hepburn, films of"), the original Genesis story does not necessarily mention a rib. The Hebrew word for the body part that God takes from Adam is *tsela*. But this word never means "rib" anywhere else in the Bible. It usually means "side," as in the side of a hill[1] or the side of a structure like the ark of the covenant,[2] the tabernacle,[3] or an altar.[4] In architecture, it refers to a side room or cell.[5] It is also used for the planks or boards in a building wall[6] and for rafters or ceiling beams.[7] The common idea in all these different meanings seems to be that of a tangent or branch extending out from a central structure or body. Given this basic sense, Adam's *tsela* would seem to refer to a "limb" or "appendage"—something that jutted out from his body.

So where did the "Adam's rib" interpretation come from? The answer is the Septuagint. The Septua-what? The Septuagint (sep-TOO-a-jent) is the name of the Greek translation of the Hebrew Bible that was done in the third century BCE. The Septuagint translated the Hebrew word *tsela* with the Greek word *pleura*, which means "side" or "rib." (It's the word from which we get "pleurisy," an inflammation in the lining of the lung. Isn't that pleasant?)

Another problem with the traditional translation of *tsela* as "rib" is that it doesn't serve the etiological agenda of the Genesis passage. Yes, we just used the word "etiological." We're not smarter than you, we just hang around words like this for a living because we're college professors. An etiology is simply a story that explains the origin of something. It may explain a biological fact, a geological formation, a social custom, or the like. The story of Adam and Eve is full of etiologies. The very name "Adam" means "man/human," and "Eve" means "life." The story explains where humans came from. It also explains such things as why snakes crawl, why people wear clothes, and why women have labor pains. The reference to a man leaving his parents to join with his wife is an etiology for marriage.

(Now that you know what an etiology is, don't get superior about it. If it comes up in dinner conversation, politely explain the meaning, just as we have here, without making your listeners feel backward and uneducated. Remember, there was a time just, oh, two minutes ago, when you didn't know the meaning of "etiology" either.)

Why does etiology matter to us here? Because the reader of the Bible expects the creation of woman from some part of man to tell a story as well. We want to know what it means, or what it explains about life as we know it. The traditional interpretation of the "Adam's rib" story included an etiology, and perhaps you have heard it. It says that God created Eve from Adam's rib, which explains why girls have one more rib than boys. At least some of you readers have undoubtedly believed that for an embarrassingly long time. But we (and the American Medical Association) are here to tell you that it is not true. It is what highfalutin university types might call a "false etiology." If you don't believe us, count your ribs, if your figure and present location allow. Now count the ribs of someone nearby who is of the opposite gender (but only if this will not get you sued for sexual harassment—see our disclaimer*). Or simply consult a trusted medical book (okay, fine—the Internet) and you will find that men and women have exactly the same number of ribs. They always have, and people in biblical times would have known it. (They could count ribs too, and back then nobody sued for sexual harassment.) If there is an etiology, or explanatory story, in the creation of Eve, it has nothing to do with rib numbers.

What makes the understanding of *tsela* as "rib" even more peculiar in the context of the Genesis story is that it does not relate to any of the obvious sexual features that distinguish men and women from one another. Yet this story is full of allusions to human sexuality. The first pair are naked and unashamed[8] until they eat of the forbidden fruit. Then their eyes are opened, and they recognize that they are naked. They immediately cover their genitals with fig-leaf aprons.[9] Given the sexually rich nature of this context, readers naturally expect that the creation of woman from man might involve some physical characteristic that is clearly different between the two.

There is another puzzling feature of the story that needs to be explained. It's not clear what it means when it says that God closed up with flesh the place where Adam's *tsela* had been. Again, considering the etiological (explanatory) nature of the story, this statement seems intended to explain the existence of some suture- or scar-like mark on the torsos of human males that is not found on females. But there is no such mark on males—at least not near their ribs.

---

*Don't count people's ribs without their permission.

Splitting the Adam and Other
Alternative Interpretations

Because of these difficulties, some interpreters through the ages have preferred to understand the word *tsela*—"side"— in different ways. Early rabbis in particular sought out alternative explanations.[10] Some of them theorized that "side" means a face (front side) or a tail (back side), which God used as a starting point to make Eve.

Other rabbis, somewhat more creatively, took the statement that God created "male and female"[11] to mean that the first human was androgynous, that is, having both male and female characteristics. They believed that the creation of Eve was nothing more than splitting apart the male and female halves of the first human. God separated the two "sides" of this bizarre him-her being, giving each new person a separate back. Thus, the first distinct man and the first distinct woman were actually created at the same time. This interpretation is popular with some modern feminists, since the simultaneous creation of man and woman implies their equality.[12] One recent feminist scholar, for instance, has theorized that "side" may mean "belly" or "womb," so that woman was created by separating the womb from the androgynous creature and using it as the beginning point for the formation of the woman.[13]

A New Solution

But these interpretations have their own problems and don't fully solve the questions we've raised. A more intriguing and satisfying new interpretation of the word *tsela* in this story comes from a

Hebrew Bible scholar named Ziony Zevit, who teaches at the American Jewish University in Los Angeles, California.[14] Zevit points out the problems with the traditional interpretation that we have just noted. Then he suggests that *tsela* might refer not to a rib but to the "baculum." Those of you in the veterinary sciences already know what we are talking about, but the rest of you should brace yourselves because "baculum" is just a fancy way of saying "penis bone." (Penis bone, penis bone, penis bone. Get used to it. The rest of the chapter is about it.) The penis bone is an actual, nonmetaphoric bone, like the bones found in your leg or hand, but it is located in the penis. Most mammals and almost all primates have a penis bone. But by some weird coincidence, only spider monkeys and human males lack one. That's right, if you are a human (or a highly literate spider monkey) male, you have no penis bone. You depend solely on hydraulics, and perhaps a prescription pharmaceutical, for your erections.

Ancient Israelites, Zevit observes, would have known that male animals possess a penis bone and that human males do not, because they would have commonly seen both human and animal skeletons—animals in the field and humans after decomposition in cave-like tombs. This is another way that ancient people also would have been well aware that women have the same number of ribs as men. In fact, they were probably more aware of this than modern people. (When was the last time *you* saw an exposed human skeleton? *CSI* doesn't count.)

Suddenly, with the penis bone difference, we have the makings of a satisfactory etiology. If Adam is lacking one particular part that all other male mammals (aside from spider monkeys) possess, and if observation clearly shows that human males have no baculum, then, like Zevit, we may allow that the story in Genesis accounts for this difference by explaining that God removed Adam's penis bone in order to make Eve from it.

Here's another brick in the wall. The Hebrew verb that describes God's creation of Eve literally means "to build." The image seems to be that of piecing together bones and other body parts to create Eve rather than forming her out of clay, as in the creation of the man and the animals. As Zevit further observes, there are no other stories or myths from the ancient world in which a rib serves a reproductive function. And of course, ribs do not exercise that function naturally. The penis, on the other hand, is obviously a generative organ in reality as well as in myth and story.

As strange as Zevit's proposal might sound initially, he finds further support for it in other details of the Bible's story. The statement that God closed up with flesh the place from which he had taken Adam's *tsela* could be a way of explaining the "raphe" on the underside of the penis and scrotum in human males. A raphe is a seam joining two parts of a bodily organ. Everyone has a raphe on the roof of the mouth. You can feel it with your tongue and see it in a mirror. Men have an additional raphe on the penis. Again, ancient Israelites would have known about this seam, and the story in Genesis explains how it got there. After God removed Adam's penis bone to create Eve, he closed over the flesh again, leaving the raphe, or "surgery scar."

Another point Zevit makes in support of his new interpretation is Adam's own comment when he sees Eve that she is "bone of my bones and flesh of my flesh."[15] This may simply be the man's way of recognizing the woman as his true kin, as opposed to the animals, who were a lot of fun but didn't possess Eve's particular *je ne sais quoi*. Indeed, later on in Genesis, when Laban discovers that he and Jacob are related, he tells Jacob, "You are my bone and my flesh."[16]

He means, "We are family." Or Adam's "bone of my bones" line may be a natural outburst of ecstasy at finally meeting someone with whom he can have sex, spend time, go to the movies, and do all the other things God made people to do together. This fits with the etiology (story meaning) for marriage, which explains that a man leaves his parents and joins his wife to become "one flesh." To reinforce this point, Adam even makes a pun on the Hebrew words for woman (*ishshah*) and man (*ish*), which is similar to the play between the English words "wo-man" and "man." In other words, "We're the same, and yet we're different. How exciting! Let's see if we can make the nine o'clock show."

But the expression "bone of my bones, flesh of my flesh" fits particularly well with Zevit's interpretation of this story. Zevit observes that there is no single word for "penis" in biblical Hebrew. Instead, the Bible uses several different words as euphemisms for the male organ; *tsela* may be one of these. "Bone" would be another one. Specifically, it would refer to the penis bone observed in other animals and once possessed by Adam but taken from him as the starting material for the creation of Eve.

The word "flesh" also sometimes refers to the penis in the Hebrew Bible. Many of these references pertain to the practice of circumcision.[17] Ezekiel, for instance, speaks of non-Israelites as being uncircumcised in heart and "flesh."[18] In another book, priests are commanded to wear undergarments to cover their naked "flesh."[19] In yet another passage dealing with bodily discharges, the word "flesh" is translated as "member."[20]

A couple of references to "flesh" in Ezekiel are almost obscene—so of course we thought we'd share them with you. Both refer to the Egyptians as being well endowed sexually. In one case, the Egyptians are said to be "great of flesh."[21] To match the crudeness of that remark, we would have to translate it as "well hung." (One popular Bible translation, the New Revised Standard Version [NRSV], waters this down by translating it as "lustful." Prudes.) The other Ezekiel reference compares the "flesh" of the Egyptians to donkey penises and adds that their "emission was like that of stallions."[22] Yes, we are still quoting from the Bible.

The Advantages and Appeal of Zevit's Interpretation

Because people are so accustomed to the traditional interpretation, Zevit's proposal may seem far-fetched at first. But on closer examination, it has some compelling advantages over other interpretations, especially the traditional one. Its suggestion about the meaning of *tsela* takes into consideration the basic meaning of the word as "side." It is also based on an obvious difference between men and women and between human males and those of other species that would have been easily observable to ancient Israelites. Thus, it differs both from the traditional interpretation of *tsela* as "rib," which assumes a difference between women and men that doesn't really exist, and from the outlandish proposal of the rabbis and others that the story imagines the first human as androgynous.

Zevit's interpretation therefore fits both the sexual content and the etiological nature of the story perfectly. Moreover, it explains the "place closed up with flesh," which other interpretations ignore. And it affords a fuller and more practical sense to the reference to the woman as "bone of my bones, flesh of my flesh."

Whether you find Zevit's proposal convincing or merely provocative, it is hard to deny its interpretive advantages, not to mention its sex appeal. His explanation is not bizarre, outrageous, or unreasonable. To the contrary, it solves long-standing problems with the text and its interpretations and fits the etiological context. It may not soon become the Sunday school standard, but for adults curious about what this Bible story means, it offers real possibilities.

2

‑‑‑⚬‑‑‑

Does "Knowledge of Good and Evil" Mean Having Sex?

L ET'S RETURN to the world's first and best nudist colony, the Garden of Eden. We know its two original occupants did everything naked—played horseshoes, gardened, sipped virgin daiquiris, and checked on the animals. But that doesn't answer a key question: when, precisely, did Adam and Eve start having sex?

Most of us would guess, "Within five seconds of seeing each other," but the real answer is more complicated than that. It hinges on some interesting turns in the ancient Hebrew language—a subject you now know can be quite titillating. Speaking of titillating, consider that Eve had no children until she and the man of the house left their Garden digs. Does this say something about their sexual activity, or lack of it? Let's take a look.

Rules Are Made to Be Broken

The Garden of Eden's founder—God—made only one rule, according to Genesis 2: don't eat from the tree of the knowledge of good and evil.[1] Big deal, right? (It would turn out to be a very big deal.) The only downside to rule number one was the harsh punishment for breaking it: death. The upside was that anything else Adam and Eve wanted to do was copacetic, which was quite a deal. And again, they got to do it naked. The Garden of Eden was a great place to hang out.

But human nature—ah! human nature—intervened. Why couldn't they be happy obeying rule number one? Why get so curious? It seems to us that God didn't help them any when he placed the tree of the knowledge of good and evil conspicuously in the middle of the Garden,[2] instead of, say, on the top of Mount Everest. It wasn't long before Eve and then Adam did exactly what God told them not to do. So ended the world's first nudist colony/commune/wild animal park.

Here's how it went down. The wily serpent, who must have seen the memo about rule number one, approached the woman and asked her if God had told them not to eat from any of the trees in the Garden. The woman replied that they could eat from all of the trees in the Garden except for the one in the middle of the Garden—the tree of the knowledge of good and evil. If they ate from it, they would die. "You won't die," the serpent cooed (or hissed, if you like). "God knows that when you eat from it your eyes will be opened and you will be like God,[3] knowing good from evil."[4] Keep that little phrase in mind, "knowing good from evil." It'll get a sexy twist later.

Eve liked the idea of having her eyes opened. It would go with her nails. So she ate the fruit and gave some to Adam. Adam, like any man today, ate anything that was handed to him that didn't smell three days old. And a surprising thing happened. They didn't die after all—at least not right away. Instead, the serpent's promise proved to be true: their eyes were opened, and they realized that they were naked.[5] Uh-oh. No more coed volleyball in the afternoons on the patio. Even worse, sin entered the world. And here we get to the part about sex.

Suddenly Adam and Eve had "knowledge of good and evil." But what does this little phrase mean? Most people usually assume it means that their moral sense was awakened and they now had the ability to choose between right and wrong. According to this idea, before eating the fruit, Adam and Eve were like adult-sized children in the Garden, as innocent as newborn calves. They didn't know right from wrong. They were also unaware of their own nakedness, kind of like a two-year-old after bath time. They ran here and there with no thought of the crazy parts bouncing around. This was humanity in its toddler stage.

But when they ate from the tree of knowledge of good and evil, they immediately passed through puberty into adolescence (also called early adulthood), which is characterized by self-awareness and a sense of right and wrong. They suddenly developed a conscience and became responsible for their moral choices. This explains why humans alone, in contrast to the animals, can make moral decisions. Unlike dogs, which must simply be trained to stop humping people's legs, humans can distinguish right from wrong and stop humping people's legs all on their own, one would hope.

Another, different view of the meaning of "good and evil" is that the phrase is a "merism." We are sorry to introduce this annoying little word into your vocabulary, but it is useful for our discussion, and it will help you win at Scrabble®. "Merism," which will net you a cool ten points on the little tiles, means expressing the totality of something by speaking of polar opposites or contrasting extremes. Common phrases like "from A to Z," "top to bottom," "East to West," and "young and old" are all merisms. In Genesis, "knowledge of good and evil" might be a merism that means "knowing everything." That would mean that by eating the forbidden fruit, Eve and Adam introduced humanity to the ability to cultivate knowledge, to learn and explore, and to develop wisdom and technology. That's not a bad thing, and that's what attracts some people to this interpretation. They think that humanity's full potential was unlocked by eating the fruit. Others would argue that this potential was unlocked prematurely and unwisely.

Let us illustrate it this way—and at the same time answer the pressing question that has been weighing on many readers' minds: how does this all pertain to *Star Trek*? Turn your attention to *Star Trek* episode number 126, star date of 3417.3, entitled "The Other Side of Paradise." In this classic episode, the crew of the *Enterprise* beams down to a planet where they are infected by spores from a mysterious plant. The spores render them passive and blissful. Even Spock enters into a blissful state and takes a lover. This alone makes the episode worth renting. The crew is on the verge of abandoning their mission. Then Captain Kirk's devotion to duty kicks in (doesn't it always?), and he discovers that strong emotions overcome the spores. He gradually regains his crew by inciting their emotions. In the final scene, McCoy remarks that humans have been kicked out of paradise for a second time. Kirk responds that this time they left voluntarily. (Run credits, and thank you, Gene Roddenberry, for everything.)

The point of this episode (which, like all *Star Trek* episodes, is available for sale, along with much slower-selling commentaries we've written, at our Web site, www.steveandjohn-thebiblesexguys. com), and the point of the Garden of Eden story according to this interpretation, is that human beings were not meant to live in paradise. We need challenges. We need problems to fix. We need leaky toilets, rusty gates, weedy lawns, and broken engines to give us something to do. We need a sense of accomplishment that goes beyond the satisfaction of watching *Andy Griffith Show* marathons. We need purpose. The Adam and Eve story explains these needs. It is a story about a trade-off. By eating the forbidden fruit, Adam and Eve lost immortality for themselves and for the rest of us. But they gained a measure of self-determination—the ability to learn and explore, to understand and enhance life.

It's an unconventional interpretation, but not as unconventional as the next one we'll consider. Which, of course, has to do with sex. You've been waiting. Here it is.

A Sexy Alternative

Jacob Milgrom is a well-known biblical scholar, now retired from the University of California, Berkeley. He brings a great deal of skill and, as we shall see, perhaps an overactive imagination to his research.[6] Milgrom thinks that "knowledge of good and evil" is a euphemism for having sex. He was actually willing to say this in a published paper that is full of words like "pluperfect" and "coelenterates," which is how scholars try to obscure the fact that they have overactive imaginations.

But does Milgrom pull this idea out of thin air? No. The phrase "knowledge of good and evil" is used elsewhere in the Bible, so we can see what it means. One time it refers to children as not knowing good and evil.[7] These "children" are defined as individuals who are younger than twenty years of age, and therefore presumably unmarried and sexually inexperienced.[8] (At twenty? Riiight.) In the other passage where the phrase "knowledge of good and evil" is used, an eighty-year-old man says that he can no longer discern good from evil. It is not clear at first what he means by this, except that maybe he's demented and writing poetry. He goes on to say that he has lost his capacities for tasting and hearing so that he can no longer enjoy the pleasures of good food and music.[9] In other words, he is too old to enjoy "wine, women, and song." The wine and song are explicit. By "discerning good from evil," our good friend Jacob Milgrom presumes that the writer means he (the old man in the Bible story, that is, not Milgrom) is too old to have sex.

Milgrom further supports his theory by pointing out that Eve received her name, meaning "the mother of all living," after God handed out the punishments to the snake and the two humans. This happened just before God drove the couple out of the Garden, busting up the paradise party like a beat cop.[10] Milgrom writes, "Before eating the fruit, she did not bear children—which suggests that Adam and Eve had no sexual intercourse in the Garden."[11] This sounds like a bummer situation—all look-y, no touch-y—and here we suspect that Milgrom's imagination has failed to engage. We think it's probable that the dynamic duo had sex while in the Garden. The Bible says that Adam and Eve were naked but unashamed before they ate the forbidden fruit.[12] As soon as they ate it, they realized they were naked.[13] Well, what happens when you realize you're naked, and *she's* naked, and it's just the two of you? Bing, bam, boom. It's beyond us to guess who jumped whose bones, but this must have been like getting the keys to a Lamborghini for the first time. Their powers of resistance must have been no match for the urge to try out their newly discovered pleasure buttons and levers. If Milgrom's theory has any credibility, it's got to assume they had sex in the Garden before they made their garments of fig leaves and before God discovered their disobedience and punished them. Indeed, maybe one of the reasons God made clothes for them later[14] was to curb their constant arousal. A dress made of freshly skinned sheep tends to do that.

Objections

Is Milgrom right? Does "knowledge of good and evil" mean to have sex? If we were as smart as he is, and we don't claim to be, we might make some objections to his theory. In fact, Milgrom is so smart that he anticipates possible objections and tries to head them off at the pass. The first is based on the verse following the creation of Eve, which states that a man leaves his parents and joins with his wife.[15] This statement may imply that Eve was intended from the beginning as Adam's sexual partner. But as anyone who has ever been married for more than two weeks knows, marriage is not the same as sex. (In fact, sometimes they seem totally at odds, but that's a subject for Dr. Phil's next book.)

The second objection is that the first time the Bible explicitly states that Adam and Eve had sex[16] follows their expulsion from the Garden: "Now the man knew his wife Eve, and she conceived and bore Cain. . . ." This might be interpreted to mean that they did the nasty for the first time after the Landlord evicted them for not complying with the rental agreement. As Milgrom observes, the Hebrew verb at this point literally means "to know" and thus supports his case for "*knowledge* of good and evil" having a sexual meaning. He also observes quite correctly that the Hebrew syntax here really demands that the verb be translated "Adam had known his wife Eve," making it likely that their sexual relationship took place earlier—in the Garden when they first tried out their fun parts.

The third objection is that the punishment laid upon Eve significantly increased her pain in childbirth,[17] which implies that she had the potential to bear children before she ate the forbidden fruit. Milgrom agrees that the potential was there. But he contends that sexual awareness was not. It was only with the eating of the fruit that Eve and Adam became aware of their nakedness and their sexuality and were able to be sexually aroused. Without sexual arousal, there is no sexual activity. Just ask any guy who's found himself in a doctor's office trying to give a semen sample while looking at medical equipment. As Woody Allen once wrote, having sex unaroused is like trying to stuff a clam into a parking meter.

Milgrom's opinion here clashes with the interpretation of the influential Christian saint Augustine, who wrote a lot of discouraging things about sex.[18] It was Augustine who, based on his interpretation of the Garden of Eden story, came up with the doctrine of original sin, which has had such an enormous impact on Christian history. Many people think original sin is a Bible doctrine. It's not. It's Augustine's idea, but it became a doctrine of the church. He believed (and tell us when we start sounding Catholic here) that Eve was created for the purpose of having babies. This meant that Adam and Eve probably had sex in the Garden—or at least Augustine thought they could have. But Augustine also thought that eating the forbidden fruit brought lust (which he called "concupiscence," because when you add more syllables it sounds less vulgar) into the world. In fact, Augustine wrote that lust was the original sin that was passed on to every newborn baby, including your latest bundle of joy. So Adam and Eve might have had sex in the Garden *before* they experienced lustful desire.

But Augustine's theory bumps up against this not-so-hard physical fact: a soft penis can't inseminate anyone. Being a fourth-century prude without the benefit of modern sexual openness, Augustine kept mum on how exactly an unaroused Adam was supposed to doink Eve. The best he could do was to suggest that Adam could have raised his penis just like he raised his arm. Animals—except for poor, dear spider monkeys—can have sex with or without arousal because of their penis bone. But could Adam really bang away with no arousal whatsoever? No. So Augustine's view is impossible (unless Augustine himself had a penis bone and was extrapolating from personal experience). But Milgrom's view makes sense: lust is exactly what was missing before Adam and Eve ate the fruit. They had the equipment for sexual reproduction but not the hot-blooded drive that enabled them to get it on.

There are two more possible objections to Milgrom's idea, and then we'll lay this one to rest. Note that God prohibited eating the fruit before Eve was ever created. Hmm. Why tell a man he can't have sex when there's no one to have sex with but himself? (Don't say it.) And finally, how did eating from the tree make Adam and Eve "like God,"[19] since Israel was monotheistic and the God of the Bible is not a sexual being?

Milgrom dodges these objections by appealing to the "deeper meaning" of the story—which is a scholar's way of leaving the debate early. Sex, he claims high-mindedly, was a manifestation of a larger and more profound characteristic—the creative impulse, which can be either constructive (good) or destructive (evil). The original sin led to sex in the sense of creative power, and in that way humans became like God. This might sound like blather, but Milgrom could point for further support to the birth of Cain, at which time Eve said, "I have acquired a man with Yahweh."[20] The verb "acquire" here means "create" elsewhere in the Bible, so that one could argue that sex and creativity are explicitly identified here as the same thing. Eve apparently saw herself as cooperating with God in the production of a son.

Ho hum. Not a very rousing ending from ol' Milgrom, but he tried. His equation of sex with the creative impulse may be a stretch, and we don't mean stretch marks. But overall his interpretation has real advantages. The expression "knowledge of good and evil" is used elsewhere in the Bible to mean sex. And it fits the sexually charged context of the Adam and Eve story better than other interpretations.

You may cling to the traditional notion that "knowledge of good and evil" means a moral sense or a capacity to create and explore. But if you choose to think it means sex, you have the support of at least one well-respected Bible scholar.

—*⁓*—

3

What Was Eve's Curse?

W HAT WAS EVE'S CURSE? Though we're not women, we
can think of lots of things that women might consider their
curse: housework, husbands, mothers-in-law, and ungrateful children who won't move out of the house until they're thirty-three.

But rewind for a moment. Was Eve really cursed in the Bible?
Or was she able to avoid punishment for breaking God's rule? One
feminist scholar has some unconventional ideas about the whole
Eve's-curse business. Let's revisit the Genesis story and see if she's
on target.

Curses in the Garden

According to the story in Genesis, sometime after Adam and Eve
had eaten of the forbidden fruit of the tree of the knowledge of
good and evil, they heard the sound of God strolling in the Garden.
They did what any guilty kids would do: they beat feet behind the
nearest bush. Remember that they had just noticed their fabulous

reproductive parts for the first time. They may even have just had sex, as we saw in the previous chapter. But in many ways they were still like little children—lots of energy, not a heck of a lot of wisdom. So God gave them a quick lesson in logic. Their conversation went something like this:

GOD: Where were you?

ADAM: Hiding.

GOD: Why were you hiding?

ADAM: I was naked.

GOD: How did you know you were naked?

ADAM: Oops.

GOD: You've eaten from the tree that I commanded you not to eat from, haven't you?

ADAM (experiencing his first-ever pass-the-buck instinct): It wasn't my fault. The woman you made to be with me—she gave me the fruit, so it was her fault. And you gave me the woman, so this one's kind of on you, God.

GOD (to Eve): What have you done?

EVE: It wasn't my fault. It was the snake's fault. It tricked me.

ADAM (aside): Nice, Eve. When in doubt, blame the snake. That'll stand up in court.[1]

For its part, the snake probably looked around for something lower than itself to blame, but all the other animals had (wisely) stampeded away from the crime scene to save their own skins. So God did what any responsible lawman does—he started passing out punishment to the perps. The snake's punishment was pretty straightforward.[2] "You are cursed among all the animals," God told it. Its curse was to be the only animal without legs, so that it was forced to crawl on its belly in the dirt. God also placed a special animosity between humans and snakes. If snakes frighten you, it all started here.

Adam's punishment was also straightforward.[3] Adam himself was not cursed, but the ground was cursed because of him. It would not be as fertile as before but would require intense labor to yield its produce. Ever since then, man has been unionizing to try to avoid this one.

Between cursing Adam and the snake, God addressed Eve. Her curse, as it is usually understood, was twofold: pain in childbirth and domination by men. The NRSV translation reads:

> I will greatly increase your pangs in childbearing;
> in pain you shall bring forth children,
> yet your desire shall be for your husband,
> and he shall rule over you.[4]

Wow—double whammy. But was this really a curse? Or was it, rather, a warning? Feminist interpreters hate this topic as much as they hate Hugh Hefner's brand of journalism. They point out that the Genesis story never actually uses the word "cursed" in reference to Eve. The serpent was cursed, and the earth that Adam cultivates was cursed. But the text does not directly say that Eve was cursed. (Ha!) However, feminists do recognize that God didn't exactly give Eve a door prize for breaking his rule. She was punished with the introduction of severe labor pains and in the loss of the equality of the sexes in the Garden.[5]

One feminist Bible scholar, perhaps desperate to ditch the curse once and for all, offers a new interpretation of Eve's "punishment." In an article entitled "Was Eve Cursed?" Adrien Janis Bledstein takes a new perspective on the punishment of pain in childbirth. She also sees the part about male domination more as a warning than as a punishment.[6] Let's see how much water her theory holds.

More Painful Than What?

God told Eve that he would greatly increase her pain in childbirth. But greatly increase it compared to what? The generally accepted idea has been that Eve's pain was greatly increased above what it was or what it would have been before she and Adam were kicked out of the Garden. The difficulty with this interpretation is that while Eve and Adam may have had sex in the Garden, Eve did not bear any children—at least none the Bible tells about—until Cain and Abel. And they were born after Adam and Eve had left Eden. God's promise to increase her pain in childbirth, then, would have been meaningless to Eve because she would not have had any previous experience to compare it to.

It is possible that Eve had children in the Garden before Cain and Abel. This might even explain where Cain's wife came from.[7] But the Bible does not mention any, and its narrative does not seem to allow room for previous children. God's discovery and punishment of the couple's disobedience seems to have followed very shortly after they ate the fruit. And if they only had sex after they became aware of their nakedness, then there was not time for a child to be born. Rather than assuming that the Bible left out part of the story and trying to fill in details, it may be better to turn to another standard interpretation.

That interpretation says that God increased Eve's labor pains above what the animals experienced. Animal-lovers and biologists debate whether animals experience pain in giving birth. No less a scientific authority than Carl Sagan, who apparently was also an amateur veterinarian, wrote, "So far as I know, childbirth is generally painful in only one of the millions of species on Earth: human beings."[8] Sagan explains that from an evolutionary point of view, pain in childbirth is the result of two uniquely human characteristics: brain size and bipedalism. A narrow pelvis made it possible for humans to walk on two legs and fit inside size 6 designer jeans. But the spectacular size of the human brain, compared to those of other animals, meant that shoving a big ol' head through something as unforgiving as a cervix would be very painful.

According to this interpretation, then, the story in Genesis explains why humans alone experience tremendous pain in the birth process. And this interpretation would still be valid even if animals do experience some pain or discomfort in giving birth, since God said he would "greatly increase" the pain for Eve. Also, the explanation offered in Genesis fits with what the ancient Israelites could observe. Only people, not animals, cry out when giving birth. And people typically deliver only one baby at a time, while many animals, and occasionally a nutty evangelical woman on fertility drugs, deliver litters of half a dozen or more. Whether animals actually experience pain in delivery or not, it would have seemed to ancient observers that they did not, or that their pain was minuscule compared to what humans experienced.

But Bledstein offers a third and more novel interpretation. She thinks that Eve's pain in childbirth was meant to contrast with ancient Near Eastern myths that described goddesses as giving birth painlessly after just a few days of pregnancy. Since the serpent tempted Eve by promising that she and Adam would become like

God (or like gods—the Hebrew can be read either way), this pain distinguishing her from goddesses in mythology seemed especially fitting. Eve's pain, then, was greatly increased over what the goddesses were said to experience.

Bledstein's interpretation is possible, if you think the story is not a strict historical account. But in the world of the story, Bledstein's proposal doesn't make sense. Eve would not have known any myths about goddesses bearing children. She had just been created, and those myths did not exist. The snake's temptation to her was that becoming like God would bring her knowledge of good and evil. Nothing was mentioned about painless childbirth among the gods. On top of this, Bledstein's theory suffers from a flaw in logic. In order for Eve to be tempted by the prospect of godlike painless childbirth, she would have to know what it was like to experience pain in childbirth. And since this pain was her punishment, she obviously had not experienced it yet.

Male Domination?

Bledstein offers a similarly novel interpretation of the second half of Eve's punishment, which has usually been interpreted as domination by her husband: "Your desire shall be for your husband, and he shall rule over you." Bledstein's new interpretation is based on a new reading of another passage that uses very similar language. In the Cain and Abel story, God tells Cain, "Sin is lurking at the door; its desire is for you, but you must master it."[9] Bledstein suggests changing the subject of the verb so that it reads: "You are lying at sin's door. It is desirable to you, but you can rule over it." She arrives at this reading by literally mincing words. She shifts the last letter of the word "sin" in Hebrew to the beginning of the word "lie." This is possible because the divisions between Hebrew words are not always certain. Then she proposes a similar interpretation for God's speech to Eve: "You are desirable to your husband, yet he can rule over you." According to Bledstein's proposed interpretation, God's words to Eve are not a curse or a punishment but a kind of warning: her attractiveness may lead to sexual domination or exploitation by the man, who is usually physically stronger. With one neat grammatical trick, Bledstein has turned God into Eleanor Smeal.

Unlike the first part of Bledstein's interpretation, there is not a fatal flaw of logic with this aspect. Still there are a couple of weaknesses to her theory. The first involves context. While the word "curse" is not used in God's speech to Eve, the context tells us there is a curse party going on. So it would be odd for God to merely warn Eve while cursing the snake and punishing Adam. Eve is punished with pain in childbirth in the first part of God's speech, so we expect to find a further punishment or something more about childbirth in the second part, not just a "Hey, watch out for sexual harassment" warning. In other words, it not only looks like a curse and quacks like a curse, but there are curses before and after it. Seems only fair to us to call it a curse.

The other possible weakness is that Bledstein strings together several unusual interpretations to form her view. She relies on her different understanding of God's message to Cain. That understanding is based on a new and different way of configuring the letters in the text. And finally, her interpretation requires that the final verb be read not as "he *shall* rule over you" but as "he *can* rule over you." None of these interpretations is impossible, but the more you pile on iffy interpretations, the weaker any argument becomes.

Did a Woman Write Genesis?

The main reason Bledstein wrote her article was to defend the possibility that the author of Genesis was a woman. She assumes that no woman would write a story in which Eve (and all women through her) was cursed by God to be dominated by men. But this may not necessarily be true. The Garden of Eden story may have been a popular tradition in ancient Israel. If so, its author may not have been free to change its content radically. Also, as we have seen, the story explains the origins of things that existed in the natural world and in Israelite society. The natural world has not changed greatly since then, but society has. The parts of the story that relate to social roles may be *descriptive* rather than *prescriptive*. That is, they tell us how things were in ancient Israel but not necessarily how they should be for all times and all societies. Israel was a male-dominated society, and the story explains this by having God tell Eve that Adam would "rule over" her. But this does not necessarily establish a pattern for all societies or all marriages.

That's good news for women of today. The bad news, at least in our view, is that Eve was cursed right along with Adam and the serpent.

4

Was Cain Clinically Depressed?

W HY OH WHY DID GOD create humans before he created
Prozac?

Poor Cain must have wondered this many times during his need-
lessly miserable life. Things started out so good for him. He was the
first person ever born, the big brother of all humanity, the first person, it could be argued, with a navel. Yet he let a silly squabble with
his younger brother get his goat. Instead of just daydreaming of taking revenge on his snotty little sibling, Cain followed through and
committed the world's first premeditated murder. He promptly became public enemy number one and narrowly avoided a giant man-
hunt that would have killed him.

Why did he do it? Was it sheer anger? Jealousy? Or has Cain's real
motive been misdiagnosed?

Mom Always Liked You Best

Let's start with what we know from the Bible's account.[1] Cain was a farmer, and Abel a shepherd. Both presented to God the fruits of their labor—Cain offered crops from his harvest, and Abel brought choice animals from his flock. For a reason that isn't stated in the text, God accepted Abel's gift but rejected Cain's. One translation (nrsv) puts it this way: "And the Lord had regard for Abel and his offering, but for Cain and his offering he had no regard." No explanation is given at this point.

We've already seen that many of the stories in these early chapters of Genesis explain the origin of something. (Remember Adam's penis bone? Who could forget it?) Many scholars believe the story of Cain and Abel functions in the same way. Some say it describes how sibling rivalry or fratricide originated. Others think it gives us clues to why people act violently toward others. One interesting theory says it helps explain the tensions between farmers and nomadic herders, a debate that still rages in Yemen.

Understandably, at God's response, Cain became "very angry and his countenance fell." The seeds of his crime were sown. He had motive. Now he was looking for opportunity.

But was Cain more than just "very angry"? According to Mayer Gruber, a Bible scholar who teaches at Ben-Gurion University in Israel, the answer is yes. In a study of the gestures, facial expressions, and other elements of nonverbal communication mentioned in Genesis 4, he concludes that "the classical scriptural illustration of depression is the story of Cain and Abel."[2] How does he support this idea?

The first clue is the reference to Cain's fallen countenance.[3] Gruber points out that, as in modern English, many ancient Near Eastern languages used the image of a fallen face to describe someone who is sad about something. For example, he cites a passage from an Akkadian myth called "The Descent of Ishtar," where the expression is used to describe a particularly distraught deity. "As for Papsukal, the vizier of the great gods, his countenance was fallen; his face was gloomy. Wearing a mourning garment, and with unkempt hair, Papsukal went before Sin, his father, weeping." Which goes to show that even mythological gods had their bad days.

Gruber argues that the association between a fallen face and sadness means that Cain's violent act against his brother was not motivated by anger, despite what many modern translations suggest. He tries to support this claim by appealing to the wording of the passage. Right before the mention of Cain's fallen face is another Hebrew expression that contains the verb *harah*, "to burn." This verb is frequently used with the word "nose"—as in "the nose burns"—to convey the idea that someone is angry. This undoubtedly comes from the reddening of an angry person's nose and face due to an increase in blood circulation. The English expression "his blood is boiling" probably relates to the same thing. Evidence from Akkadian, the ancient Mesopotamian language in which "The Descent of Ishtar" is told, indicates that it was not uncommon in antiquity to use the verb "to burn" to describe feelings of anger, sadness, or depression.

But in Hebrew, when the verb denotes anger, it is always used in conjunction with the nose. Gruber believes that the lack of a mention of Cain's nose means the verb has some other meaning in this story. The actual phrase is *yihar leqayin*, "it was burning to Cain." According to Gruber, when the verb is followed by the preposition *le*, as it is here, it often denotes sadness or depression. He points to the

story of Jonah: the NRSV, like many English translations, renders the
two occurrences of the verb as "to be angry," but Gruber believes
the text is actually referring to Jonah's depression:

> *When the sun rose, God prepared a sultry east wind, and the sun*
> *beat down on the head of Jonah so that he was faint and asked that he*
> *might die. He said, "It is better for me to die than to live." But God said*
> *to Jonah, "Is it right for you to be angry about the bush?" And he said,*
> *"Yes, angry enough to die."*[4]

In Gruber's view, translators and commentators often do not
make a distinction between *harah* followed by the word "nose,"
which denotes anger, and *harah* followed by the preposition *le,* which
can sometimes describe depression. "It is clear on purely philologi-
cal grounds that the story of Cain and Abel cannot be construed as
an account of the dangerous effects of ordinary anger," he writes.[5]

Gruber then offers an interpretation that, though a bit too Freudian for us, may include some truth. He says that God's rejection of
Cain's offering was the loss of a love object that resulted in a depressed state. Cain's self-esteem plummeted when his offering was
not accepted, and so in a state of dejectedness he took out his frus-
tration on the one who had received the affirmation he craved. This
led God to ask him, in Gruber's translation at least, "Why are you
depressed, and why has your face fallen?"[6]

Smile! God Loves You

Notice that God didn't leave Cain to smolder. Rather, he continued
with a follow-up question intended to shake Cain out of his funk.
Unfortunately, the next part of God's advice to Cain is incomplete

and so its meaning is obscure.[7] A literal translation would be something along the lines of "If you do well lifting up," an enigmatic phrase that the King James Version and the NRSV change to "If you do well, will you not be accepted?"

Here Gruber sees an opening. He thinks the Hebrew word for "lifting up" is meant to contrast with the reference to Cain's fallen face in the previous verse. He believes there is an ellipsis, or missing section, in the second part of the phrase that contains the word "face." According to Gruber, this lifting up of the face is a description of smiling, the opposite of the fallen countenance that God has just questioned Cain about.

Gruber further proposes an additional ellipsis at the beginning of the phrase, where the word "heart" is implied as the thing that Cain "makes well." The phrase "to make the heart well" is a common biblical Hebrew expression for being happy, so this leads Gruber to conclude that the actual sense of God's question to Cain is: "Indeed, if you will make yourself happy, you will regain your smile." Gruber sees this as a divine diagnosis of Cain's depression, which, in those pre-Prozac days, could only be cured by cheering himself up.

Gruber then brings up the strangest aspect of the Cain and Abel story. The next verse of the Hebrew text begins with the words "Cain said to his brother Abel," and then it skips abruptly to "and when they were in the field, Cain rose up against his brother Abel, and killed him."[8] The NRSV, along with many other English translations, inserts the sentence "Let us go out to the field" between these two sections. These words are found in some of the ancient translations, like the Greek and Syriac, but the original Hebrew doesn't record them.

Gruber cites this break in the flow of the story as indicating a breakdown in communication between the brothers. This non sequitur underscores how irrational Cain's act of murder was. According to Gruber, the violent act came out of nowhere, and its randomness is best understood as a result of Cain's state of despair. Following the typical trajectory of one who was battling depression, his initial loss of self-esteem was followed by a recovery time during which his pent-up emotions were directed outward against those closest to him. "He becomes depressed; he cannot hold his head up; he cannot be talked out of his depression, which, according to psychoanalytic theory, is anger at his lost love-object turned inward upon himself. Apparently Cain regains his self-esteem and releases aggressive impulses against his only sibling, Abel."[9]

Raising Cain

What do we make of Gruber's depressed Cain? It is persuasive in its analysis of the story's vocabulary, particularly the different meanings of the verb "to burn" depending on whether the word "nose" is used with it. Because there is no reference to Cain's nose, Gruber is quite right that it is a mistake to translate the verb "to be angry" as many English versions do. This, combined with his observations about the use of the expression "fallen face" to convey the idea of sadness, suggests that Cain's state of mind was closer to depression than anger when God chose Abel's gift over his.

Depression also makes sense on a commonsense level. Who wouldn't be depressed and confused if God rejected their gift but happily received their brother's? The most natural thing in the world would be to slide into despondency.

Unfortunately, the text does not tell us directly what Cain was feeling. In fact, the authors of the Bible often kept mum on such particulars. That makes psychoanalyzing a character a slippery undertaking. Biblical narratives are notoriously terse, and the lack of detail makes it difficult to know for sure what's going on inside a character's head. As popular as this story is around the world, it's amazing how little we actually know about what Cain and Abel really thought.

The text's reluctance to clue us in on Cain's mental state is one reason we don't find Gruber's suggestion completely convincing. The vocabulary suggests that it's possible, perhaps likely, that Cain felt depressed after God didn't accept his offering. But what was he feeling later on when he invited Abel for a walk in the field as a ploy to kill him? Conceivably, as Gruber proposes, he could still have been sad or depressed, but it's also possible his mood had shifted to one of anger or jealousy. It could even be that he was experiencing a variety of emotions he was trying to sort through. Gruber's reconstruction is plausible, but he never clinches the argument—and indeed, the lack of information given in the text suggests that he can't.

Gruber also relies on the presence of two ellipses at a critical point in the story. He claims that the words "face" and "heart" should be inserted even though the text does not include them.[10] While ellipses are well documented in biblical Hebrew, it would be most unusual to have two so close together. And anyhow, it's not wise to make missing words the linchpin of an argument.

Ironically, Gruber then goes against scholarly consensus in the very next verse, where he dismisses the idea of there being an ellipsis.[11] Following the ancient translations, most scholars believe Cain's words to Abel should be inserted into the text to improve the narrative's flow. But Gruber prefers to see the gap as an intentional device the author uses to create a non sequitur that is yet another indication of Cain's depression. This is a forced suggestion, and by this point Gruber is playing fast and loose with the text, perhaps in an attempt to salvage his theory.

We can't know for sure whether Cain was depressed or just nursing a grudge against Abel, but Gruber's arguments do help readers get inside the mind of the world's first murderer and consider his motivations with a little more depth.

5

Does the Bible Encourage Us to Drown Our Sorrows in Beer?

IF YOU DESPISE YOUR LIFE and find this absurd drama we're in to be meaningless, welcome to the Bible's Book of Ecclesiastes. It's more hopeless than a Russian novel, more depressed than the Angolan stock market. After reading it, even a trip to your local mortuary would seem cheery.

But this biblical handbook of pessimism does include a bright spot for beer-lovers. After surveying all the wisdom of man, the author finally comes to this conclusion: let's all kick back with a cold one.

Count us in. But first, let's look at a beer-y theory involving Ecclesiastes, the only Bible book to heartily endorse hitting the local bar.

In Vino Veritas

Ecclesiastes is one of the Hebrew Bible's three "wisdom writings," along with Proverbs and Job. Each is a product of the Israelite wisdom tradition, which attempted to address life's big questions with more depth than the usual gaggle of ancient Jewish college students having a late-night bull session. Proverbs is a collection of aphorisms and maxims that offer insights about how the world works and give instruction on how to live. The Book of Job, another gun-to-the-head type of read, explores the problem of innocent suffering and God's role in it.

But for misery, the Book of Ecclesiastes outdoes them all. It contains the musings of an ancient Woody Allen type resigned to the absurdity and emptiness of life. The book is actually called "Qoheleth," which refers to the title by which the author was known. The word "Qoheleth" comes from a Hebrew root that means "to gather," and it could be a reference to the great wisdom or possessions that this man known as Qoheleth accumulated during his lifetime. A few passages in the book claim that Qoheleth was the king of Israel.[1] Some think this was a literary device to increase sales in Mesopotamia (like your writing a book and putting "written by the President of the United States" on the cover).

In spite of Qoheleth's great wisdom and/or riches, his philosophy of life was as bleak as Beckett's: "We're born, we die, we're forgotten." He saw life as a random series of events. Nothing about it was fair. Some people have relatively good lives. They get to live in America and read humorous books about naughty Bible stories and drink specialty coffees whose price could feed a child in Africa for a month. Other people aren't so lucky. They end up being that child in Africa who goes hungry because American readers prefer double lattes and light literary amusement. Meanwhile, all across the planet good people suffer bad things and bad people are rewarded. Human existence is a cycle of despair and anxiety set in motion by an inscrutable, disinterested God. Now you know why Qoheleth is considered the rightful father of the French cinema. Here's a comfortless sample of his opinions:

> What has been is what will be, and what has been done is what will be done; there is nothing new under the sun.[2]

> For there is no enduring remembrance of the wise or of fools, seeing that in the days to come all will have been long forgotten. How can the wise die just like fools?[3]

> And I thought the dead, who have already died, more fortunate than the living, who are still alive; but better than both is the one who has not yet been, and has not seen the evil deeds that are done under the sun.[4]

> For no one can anticipate the time of disaster. Like fish taken in a cruel net, and like birds caught in a snare, so mortals are snared at a time of calamity, when it suddenly falls on them.[5]

What's a person to do? Well, drink, of course! Our good buddy Qoheleth believed that alcohol is a remedy for the boredom and monotony of the human condition. He wrote, "This is what I have seen to be good: it is fitting to eat and drink and find enjoyment in all the toil with which one toils under the sun the few days of the life God gives us; for this is our lot."[6] Hear, hear, say we. Indeed, "Eat, drink, and be merry" is Ecclesiastes' common refrain and serves as a drawstring to tie together the entire book.

But one scholar is not satisfied with the explicit permission to drink. He claims to have uncovered a hidden reference to beer in Ecclesiastes. Does his interpretation give us one more for the road, or a serious hangover?

Beer Here!

The passage in question reads: "Throw your bread upon the face of the water, because in many days you will acquire it. Give a serving to seven and also to eight, because you do not know what evil will be upon the land."[7]

In a brief article published in 2002, Michael M. Homan, a professor at Xavier University of Louisiana, maintains that this passage is speaking about beer.[8] He explains that bread played an important role in the production of beer in the ancient Near East. Baked dough made of germinated cereals was put in jars of water that also contained yeast, and the maltose sugars would eventually convert to alcohol. (Bet you didn't know this book came with a quick recipe for home brew.) Homan suggests that Qoheleth's instruction to throw bread on the water was an allusion to the beer-making process.

His idea goes against traditional interpretations. Many commentators think that "throwing your bread upon the water" is a call to be generous, because in the karmic circle of things your generosity will be rewarded someday. A number of extra-biblical legends make the same point, and some appear to be associated with this passage. Homan cites one legend about a man who wanted to test the truth of this passage, so each day he put his name on hundreds of loaves of bread and tossed them into the ocean. Before his neighbors could throw him into an insane asylum, some of the loaves reached the son of the Muslim leader Mutawakkil of Baghdad, who had become trapped under a rock while swimming. He was able to sustain himself with the unexpected supply of (somehow non-soggy!) bread until help arrived and he was rescued. Then the original owner of the bread was richly compensated for saving the wealthy ruler's son.

The other common interpretation of the Ecclesiastes passage sees casting one's bread upon the water as a metaphor for international commerce. In this reading, Qoheleth is encouraging people to transport their goods abroad and do business with foreigners. As Homan notes, a popular 1976 English translation of the Bible that is written in a modern colloquial style (Today's English Version, also known as "The Good News Bible") puts the passage this way: "Invest your money in foreign trade, and one of these days you will make a profit."

Homan rejects both common interpretations and, in a bald attempt to gain popularity with college students, says, "A more likely interpretation, given the process by which beer was brewed in the ancient Near East, is that Qoheleth is recommending both beer production and consumption in perilous times."[9]

Last Call

Does Homan's idea hold any water? Or beer? Or anything? At first glance, maybe. He's on solid footing to point out how important beer was in ancient cultures. Those who think the Germans invented beer during a particularly nasty winter in the 1300s will enjoy knowing that beer actually has been around longer than written language. Maybe that's why it took so long for language to develop in the first place. In fact, the Sumerians, who invented written language, also loved beer. (Funny how writing and drinking went hand in hand back then too.) The Sumerians even had a goddess of beer, Ninkasi, who must have been some righteous babe because a lengthy hymn was written to her sometime around 1800 BCE that described her involvement in and protection over every aspect of the beer-making process. We are not making this up. The hymn opens by describing Ninkasi as the one "born of the flowing water," and it ends with a celebration of the finished product. Get a load of these actual words from this ancient poem: "When you pour out the filtered beer of the collector vat, it is like the onrush of the Tigris and the Euphrates." Put that to music, add some Budweiser Girls, and you've got a cross-cultural tavern song anyone can sing to.

So beer was part of ancient society, just like it's part of ours. When you consider that people five thousand years ago probably kicked off work early to hit their favorite watering hole, you might start to agree with Qoheleth that there really is nothing new under the sun. Indeed, Homan observes that the text's admonition to give a serving to "seven and also to eight" reflects the important social role drinking played in the ancient world by bringing people together.

Homan's most important appeal, however, is to another one of history's ancient beer-drinking capitals, Babylon (located in the same place as Sumer, but centuries later). The Babylonians didn't have a Miller Lite Goddess, to our knowledge, but they were among the first to raise beer-making to an art form. Imagine a land dotted with microbreweries and you're probably on the right track. Homan points out that in beer-making the Babylonians used the verb "to throw" to describe the moment when the key ingredients were added to the water. Homan argues that this is precisely the meaning of the verb rendered "to cast" or "to throw" in Ecclesiastes.

Homan's second argument is that given the overall character and theme of Ecclesiastes, his interpretation fits well. He then cites other biblical texts that, he says, recommend drowning your sorrows in booze. Similar advice can also be found in other ancient Near Eastern writings.

Flat Brew

Homan's interpretation starts to smell skunky, however, when you get into the details. The semantic connection he tries to make between the verb Babylonians used for "to throw" and the Hebrew word (*shillah*) that he translates as "throw" is not as strong as it might seem. The primary meaning of the Hebrew form is "to send" or "to stretch out," with the emphasis usually on the direction in which something is being sent or the destination to which someone is being sent. Therefore, when Qoheleth urges us to cast our bread upon the water, there is an implied interest in where it will end up. There is no implication that it will sink into the water and mix with other elements to become beer. The Hebrew verb never means "to throw," and there are several common verbs with that meaning that the author could have used to convey that sense. For example, the writer of the Book of Jonah used a different Hebrew verb and preposition to describe the act of the sailors tossing Jonah overboard. Similarly, the preposition used by Qoheleth implies that the bread floats on top of the water rather than going down into it (remember the "loaf preservers" of legend?). In the game of barstool Bible trivia, Homan takes strike one.

Homan also dismisses the two usual ways of interpreting the passage too matter-of-factly, without citing compelling evidence of their shortcomings. He gives each argument a paltry one sentence in his paper. He rejects the idea that Qoheleth was calling for generosity by saying that the Arab legend of Mutawakkil's son quotes the Qoheleth passage but that this doesn't affect the meaning of the Qoheleth text. He then challenges the view that the passage endorses foreign trade by arguing that the word for "bread" never means "merchandise." This is true, but the word is used a number of times in a metaphorical way, as in "bread of tears" and "bread of adversity," so it is conceivable that it could be functioning similarly here even if the qualifier ("success" or "hard work," for example) is unexpressed. To definitively refute these interpretations Homan needs to give them a more thorough whipping, not the casual brush-off. Strike two.

Next, the word "serving" in Homan's translation of the passage ("Give a serving to seven and also to eight") subtly reinforces the association with beer he wishes to stress, but it is not the most common way the Hebrew term *heleq* ("serving") is translated. A *heleq* typically designates a portion of something that is either taken by someone or given to someone to possess. It is commonly used in the Hebrew Bible to refer to booty taken in war or land that is divided up and parceled out. While it is sometimes used in reference to food, as might be the case here, it never describes a measure of water or any other drink. This does not totally destroy Homan's suggestion, but it weakens its likelihood. We'll call this ball one.

Homan finally goes down swinging in trying to find support for beer-drinking elsewhere in the Bible. One passage he cites is Isaiah 22:13. Taken by itself, this verse does seem to endorse the carpe-diem attitude Homan describes because it contains the words "let us eat and drink, for tomorrow we die." But read in context, the passage's meaning is the exact opposite of what Qoheleth was saying. The prior verses make it clear that the prophet was quoting people who disregarded God's command to adopt a more somber lifestyle during a time of crisis. "In that day the Lord GOD of hosts called to weeping and mourning, to baldness and putting on sackcloth; but instead there was joy and festivity, killing oxen and slaughtering sheep, eating meat and drinking wine." Unlike Qoheleth, Isaiah said that drinking was not an acceptable response to life's difficulties.

The same can be said of another alleged beer text Homan relies on. This is part of a brief section of the Book of Proverbs in which King Lemuel, who is otherwise unknown, was getting advice from his mother. In this verse, dear old Mom told her son to "give strong drink to one who is perishing, and wine to those in bitter distress."[10] But this was to be done only to alleviate their pain and misery. Earlier she warned the king about the dangers of strong drink, which can fog the mind and dull the senses. A responsible person, particularly one in a position of authority like Lemuel, must lay off the hooch because it hampers one's ability to function effectively.

Homan's claim that these two texts correspond to Qoheleth's message is flatly incorrect because they actually caution against drinking. The eat-drink-and-be-merry theme found throughout Qoheleth does not extend to other parts of the Hebrew Bible. This shows how unique and unusual Qoheleth is among the biblical writings.

As noted briefly already, Homan also tries to defend his reading of Ecclesiastes 11:1–2 by appealing to other ancient Near Eastern proverbs that extol the benefits of drinking to deal with life's problems. Our response to this is a scholarly "Big whoop." The existence of other proverbs only demonstrates that people in neighboring civilizations were thinking about the same things and reaching the same conclusions about life. There is no connection between the texts other than a generally shared sentiment about the human condition. You can't force outside meanings onto a biblical text in which that sentiment is not clearly stated.

We spent a long time debating Homan's arguments, and the higher the bar tab got the more convinced Steve became. But the next morning John reminded him that just because you propose a clever possibility does not make it so. Unfortunately, Homan's interpretation is several cans short of a six-pack. It is not impossible that Ecclesiastes 11:1–2 makes an oblique reference to beer production, but it's also not impossible that through genetic engineering one day pigs will fly. And anyway, why would Qoheleth hide his meaning here when throughout the rest of the book he openly advocated drinking? Anyone seeking unambiguous biblical support for happy hour only has to thumb through the rest of Ecclesiastes, which remains the only book in the canon to function, at least in part, like a beer advertisement.

6

Did Abraham Pimp Sarah?

ABRAHAM IS PERHAPS the single most admired man in history and holds a vaunted position in three of the world's great religions: Christianity, Judaism, and Islam. Many of the events of his life, like the near-sacrifice of his son Isaac, are among the Bible's best-known stories. Abraham's deep faith and commitment to God have inspired generations of believers, and many look to him as a model of good behavior.

But on the way to becoming the patriarch of three faiths, Abraham twice behaved like nothing more than an inner-city pimp. In these instances, he had his wife Sarah pose as his sister, opening up the possibility that she would have sex with another man.[1] To make matters worse, Abraham's son Isaac proved to be a chip off the old block when he later tried to do the same thing to his wife Rebekah.[2]

Why did these patriarchs do that? Were they really afraid of being killed by the local king, as they claimed to be? Or were greater forces at work that played upon this story in unexpected ways, causing these men to act out hidden fantasies?

A Family Affair

In the first version of this story, Abraham, called by his shorter name, Abram, left his homeland in modern-day Iraq and obeyed God's command to journey to the land of Canaan.[3] Because of a famine, he didn't stay there long before heading to Egypt with Sarah (whose name at this time was Sarai). Before reaching their destination, Abraham convinced his wife to pass herself off as his sister. He did this for self-preservation—Abraham was afraid the Egyptians would be captivated by Sarah's beauty and decide to kill him so they could have her for themselves. But if they thought she was his sister, his life would be spared and things would "go well with me because of you," as he told Sarah.

Abraham's plan worked to perfection. When Pharaoh, the king of Egypt, saw Sarah, he took her into his house and heaped all kinds of gifts on her "brother" Abraham. But Abraham didn't stop to consider what God's reaction to his ruse would be. In an impressive display of what seems to be misplaced divine anger, God sent plagues on Pharaoh, who somehow connected the dots and confronted Abraham about what he had done. Then Pharaoh sent Abraham and Sarah on their way.

Provocatively, this story never dishes on the question of "Did they or didn't they?" Pharaoh took Sarah as his wife, which leads us to assume that they had sexual relations. But it is never explicitly stated in the story. The truth hides behind the curtain of history, and readers are still left to wonder.

There is no such ambiguity in the second version, where Abraham tried the same trick on another foreign ruler, King Abimelech of

Gerar.[4] This time God intervened before Abimelech could touch Sarah and informed him of Abraham's ploy. When the king asked Abraham for an explanation, Abraham admitted that he feared for his life, as he did earlier with Pharaoh, but then he went on to make a shocking revelation—he and Sarah shared the same father! We're not sure if this makes the situation better or worse. Technically, he did not lie, but marrying your sister? Eeeww. Echoing Pharaoh's generosity eight chapters earlier, Abimelech bestowed gifts of animals and slaves upon Abraham and invited him to settle anywhere in Gerar.

A generation later, Isaac continued the sordid family tradition when he told the men of Gerar that his wife Rebekah was his sister in order to save his own skin.[5] This time the "sister" didn't even make it to the king's house. Abimelech, who is identified as "king of the Philistines," happened to observe the couple engaging in sexual play and he became furious with Isaac for creating a situation that would have allowed an improper sexual encounter between one of his men and Rebekah.

The Troubling Questions

Whoever first said that bad news always comes in threes might have had these stories in mind. For us and other scholars, these episodes bring up several troubling questions:

1. *Why did the patriarch think he was in danger?* There is nothing in the stories to suggest that any of these foreign rulers wanted to kill, or even harm, Abraham and Isaac. In fact, each time the deception was revealed, the response was just the opposite: the king was generous or wished Abraham or Isaac well. Abraham's and Isaac's initial paranoia that their

wives' beauty would lead to their own destruction proved to be entirely without merit.

2. *Didn't the patriarch care about what would happen to his wife?* By masquerading as her brother, each man virtually guaranteed that his wife would be taken into another man's house. It appears that Abraham and Isaac were only afraid of what might happen to themselves, not to the women. Their survival instinct had completely taken over, and they subjected Sarah and Rebekah to whatever situations they might encounter in another man's house. This is a particularly poignant issue because in the second version Abraham had just received word from God that Sarah would conceive and have a son. For all he knew, she might already be pregnant, but this didn't seem to factor into his decision.

3. *Why did we not hear from the wife?* Sarah and Rebekah are central to the plots of the narratives, but they remain completely silent throughout all three episodes. We are not even told what they were thinking as their husbands asked them to lie for them. Actually, "ask" is too kind a word. Abraham didn't request Sarah's assistance—he demanded it: both times his words to her were put in the imperative form: "Say you are my sister." Isaac did his father one better. He didn't even try to coerce Rebekah into joining the charade. Maybe he was afraid she would blow her line. Instead, he boldly declared to the men of Gerar, "She is my sister." Apparently neither woman had a vote or a voice.

4. *Why is the story repeated three times?* It is rare if not unique in the Bible to have three such similar stories so close to each other, let alone occurring within the same family. These are

indeed the only stories in the whole Bible in which a man tries to pimp his wife. Upon closer inspection, there appears to be a progression in how the scenes are presented: the first time it appears that Sarah had sexual relations with the foreign ruler; the second time she was brought into his house, but they were not physically intimate; and the third time Rebekah did not even get in the door because the king spied the couple and discovered the truth.

Is this arrangement intentional? What do we make of all this outlandish behavior?

Abraham on the Couch

Such questions have attracted the interest of Bible scholars for a long time, and typically they have tried to address only one or two of these issues without proposing a comprehensive solution that might explain them all. Dominating these discussions have been questions like: Which story is the oldest? Why are they different? And how do they compare ethically?

Then along came J. Cheryl Exum, a well-known professor of Bible at the University of Sheffield in England. She offers an entirely different approach to the question.[6] Exum thinks that the characters of Abraham, Isaac, and Jacob reflect the deep-seated motivations of a male narrator to—yes—encourage his wife to have sex with someone else. This will take some 'splaining.

Unlike many other scholars, Exum views the three stories as parts of a whole rather than as separate, unrelated units. The method Exum adopts is quite unusual, at least by the normal standards of biblical scholarship. She offers a psychoanalytical reading that tries to illuminate what she calls the "narrative unconscious" of the text. Her conclusion is that these stories all address the secret fantasy lurking in a man's mind that his wife will have sex with another man. In Exum's words, "Because there is something fearful and attractive to the (male) narrator about the idea of the wife being taken by another man, a situation that invites the woman's seizure is repeated three times. . . . Telling the story of the patriarch's repetitive behavior offers the occasion for a 'working out' of the neurosis."[7]

In Exum's view, this explains why Abraham and Isaac come up with a plan that ensures that their wives will have sex with other men. This is precisely what they want to happen. Seen in this way, the stories are about the desire and fear of the narrator. He desires to have his choice of the woman validated, and this will happen if another man finds her attractive. If the other man tries to take her, this might even increase the husband's desire for her. At the same time, there is an element of fear. Sexual relations with another man will give the woman a point of comparison. The other guy might have read *The Joy of Sex* and therefore be a better lover. Maybe the woman will enjoy his bedroom tricks. According to Exum, these stories are an attempt to resolve the thoughts and feelings that have their origin in the man's hidden fantasy that his wife will be taken by another man.

Note what Exum is not saying. She does not believe that the stories reflect the unconscious of a particular individual, like Abraham or Isaac. Rather, she speaks of a collective, male-centered unconscious, whose spokesperson she calls "the narrator." She sees the texts as communal products that were given their final shape by males. The psychology and mind-set of the stories therefore inevitably reflect those of their male authors and editors, in her view.

Exum proposes that we think of the characters as split-off parts of the narrator. Just as when a person under analysis is able to recognize aspects of himself or herself in the various characters of a dream, the characters in the Genesis stories are vehicles that allow the biblical narrator to work out the neurosis he is experiencing. In order to interpret the movement from one version of the story to the next, Exum adopts a Freudian model that makes use of his famous three-part division of the human psyche. Exum throws out lots of ids, egos, and superegos in her scholarly paper, but we'll try to sum them up neatly and quickly.

In the first story, Pharaoh functions as the superego, which monitors a person's actions to ensure that they are not immoral. Abraham, with his unconscious desire to hand over Sarah to another man, is the id, which seeks to act out repressed fantasies and desires. The text, according to Exum, is the ego, where these conflicting impulses are worked out and Pharaoh takes Sarah as his wife.

The second version advances the psychological drama by allowing Abimelech (the superego) to justify himself before God, who functions as the external moral law. This explains why the king proclaims his innocence when God chastises him in a dream for almost taking Sarah for himself. Similarly, Abraham (the id) justifies his deceit to Abimelech (the superego) by pointing out that he did not lie since he and Sarah share the same father. Abraham even tries to blame the external moral law for his predicament by pointing a finger at God for making him leave his father's house in the first place. As Exum points out, if Abraham had been truly innocent, he probably wouldn't have protested as much as he did.

By the time we reach the third version, the superego functions independently of outside influence and constraints. The king sees for himself that the couple is in fact married, and so he avoids even the suggestion of impropriety. The fascination with the fantasy has been abandoned since the men of Gerar are not interested in Rebekah, even though she and her husband have been among them for a "long time." Isaac (the id) has finally worked through the neurosis that has been a preoccupation since chapter 12, and he is able to enjoy conjugal relations with his wife after resolving the problem. As Exum points out, the patriarch ultimately feels like the winner of a contest. "Having Abimelech, the rival, witness his sexual activity with the matriarch is the patriarch's ultimate turn-on, his incontestable victory over his rival desire."[8]

Examining the Proposal

As out of left field as Exum's psychological interpretation might seem, it adequately addresses all four of the questions we posed earlier. It explains why the patriarch thinks he is in danger: his fear is displaced. He secretly desires that his wife be taken by another man, but fears the result. It also explains why the patriarch doesn't seem to care what will happen to his wife. In Exum's reading, he cares deeply—perhaps so deeply that he doesn't even realize it. The twist is that what he wants to happen to her is not the kind of thing men normally acknowledge, even if many of them share Abraham's and Isaac's fantasy that their wife will be taken by another man.

Exum's proposal also resolves the question of why we don't hear from Sarah and Rebekah—this is a guy thing. The male psychology and mind-set that created the stories are just not interested in developing the woman's character in the narratives beyond her role as a sex object. Finally, Exum explains why we have three different versions of the same story and why they are in this order. They express three different moments of a psychological movement from imagining the fantasy to rejecting it. The order shows the resolution of a psychological problem.

This interpretation also has the advantage of preserving the integrity of the text as we have it and not requiring that we appeal to different sources to explain the repetition of the story.

We'll have plenty more to say about Exum's approach in a later chapter. But for now it's worth pointing out that, make of it what you will, Exum has done a fine job of answering the questions Bible scholars like to ask about this passage.

7

Was the Toilet Ehud's
Escape Hatch?

W E HAVEN'T DEALT YET WITH POOP, so we're excited to finally get to this chapter. This next case of "Is that really in the Bible?" reads like a TV crime drama script infused with tasteless details by a potty-obsessed five-year-old. If the movie *Psycho* kept a generation of people from taking showers for fear of being stabbed by Norman Bates, this chapter may accomplish the same thing for latrines.

Like us, you may have at one time or another experienced that primal human fear of being killed on the toilet. (Ever read Stephen King's *Dreamcatcher*?) Perhaps it's simply a feeling of vulnerability as you crouch there defenseless—or perhaps those fears are grounded in something much more real. Biblical history, for example. Most of us have had unpleasant experiences on the toilet. But as bad as your experiences have been, a Bible guy named Eglon had it much worse. He was killed on his way to the "throne." As we'll see, this story, like many in the Bible, flouts modern good taste with real flair. Listen closely—that giant flushing you hear is the sound of our scholarly reputations going down the pipes. Now let's get to the straight poop.

Murder Most Foul

This story is told in the Book of Judges. Judges were rulers who led Israel almost like kings, and they ruled by fiat (as some U.S. judges still do). The story we are dealing with here is not the longest or most widely known story in the Book of Judges—that honor goes to Samson and Delilah—but after seeing what unfolds, you may never forget these vivid details. Ehud's contributions to Israelite history are recapped in a slight nineteen verses that describe just one episode, but it's a doozy.[1]

Let's reconstruct the crime scene. It was a normal day in the Middle East. Moabites were plotting to kill Israelites; Israelites were plotting to kill Moabites. Both dreamed of assassinating each other's kings. As it is today, the Middle East was one big, happy family.

On this day, the king of Moab, named Eglon (or Fatty, if you like), took a magazine and headed for his favorite room in the house. He had reason to feel content. He was successfully oppressing the Israelites. He had plenty of food. In fact, the name "Eglon" means "young calf." Eglon was living up to his name. Though the Bible rarely describes people's physical traits, it goes out of its way to say that Eglon "was exceedingly fat." Either the historian who put these words to goatskin was feeling a bit cheeky that day, or King Eglon's weight problem would factor into the plot. We'd bet on the latter.

While the pleasant day unfolded at the palace of King Fatty, another person entered—Ehud, or Lefty, because the text says he was "left-handed." (In another example of Bible humor that you only get

if you spend endless years studying ancient Hebrew, Ehud is identified as "of the tribe of Benjamin." The name "Benjamin" means
"son of the right hand," so this is like saying, "Lefty, son of Righty."
This would have had the ancient copyists rolling.) In came Lefty to
the palace of King Fatty, who was working up a good dump in the
upper chambers (we are not being gratuitous; this is actually part
of the plot). Okay, the nicknames were fun, but to avoid confusion,
let's go back to the real names. Ehud ("Lefty") had brought with him
an eighteen-inch double-edged knife, strapped to his right leg, and
a gift. He was welcomed into the king's chambers, where he gave
King Eglon the gift. But Ehud apparently forgot to think up a good
method for getting the king alone so he could kill him. ("Hey, let's
you and me go in the other room and have a bon-bon-eating contest"
didn't come to mind, but probably would have worked.) Instead,
Lefty laid on King Fatty the most hackneyed line in crime drama history: "I have a secret message just for you." Even preadolescent fans
of mob movies could have sniffed that one out.

But Eglon, whose BS antenna must have been broken, was completely suckered by this. He eagerly dismissed his servants, and Ehud
proceeded to the king's "cool roof chamber," where he was sitting
on his throne. Without wasting any time, Ehud seized the knife
with his left hand (naturally) and thrust it into the unsuspecting
Eglon's belly—here's your message, Tub-o!—where it completely
disappeared, enveloped in folds of fat. Eglon was not only too fat
to dodge the blow, but he was now actually hiding his own murder
weapon. With visions of the healthier lifestyle he never pursued
running through his head, Eglon keeled over—and defecated! How's
that for drama: not just blood and guts, but good old-fashioned crap.
The shock of the attack must have loosened the poor man's sphinc-
ters, and he dropped his payload. Ehud, apparently deciding to leave
the knife stuck in the king rather than fish around for it with the

awful stench taking over the room, locked the doors to the king's chamber and escaped the murder scene, cool as a cucumber.

The king's servants, clearly the worst bodyguards in Moabite history, decided not to check on their boss for a long time. Apparently that familiar odor that said, "Eglon wuz here," was emanating from his room. Assuming that he was on his preferred throne relieving himself, they went back to playing the ancient Moabite version of pinochle. Nobody, it seems, was eager to check on him. Perhaps the palace help always abandoned the building when Eglon felt the call of nature. But finally, after an embarrassingly long time, the servants got worried. No magazine was that long. They got the key and opened the locked door, only to discover the king sprawled dead on the floor and an awful mess that someone would have to clean up. Ehud, meanwhile, was long gone. Later that day he led his fellow Israelites in a rousing military victory over the demoralized Moabites, who were wondering exactly what to say in Eglon's public obituary ("Died at home surrounded by his recent works"?).

Does It Really Say That?

The story is gross. Are we embellishing it? Certainly not. The Hebrew text tells us that the king's servants actually thought Eglon was on the toilet. The text uses the slang of the day—"he is covering his feet," a Bible expression that refers to the fact that when you squat to take care of business, your clothing is usually around your ankles. (This charming little phrase is also found in 1 Samuel 24, when King Saul enters a cave to relieve himself. It was probably a little trick the writers used to ridicule kings they didn't like.)

The other key word in the disgusting panoply of facts is *parshedona*, used in verse 22, which describes something that "goes out." It doesn't take a genius—or even two Bible scholars—to recognize that this tells us that something went out of Eglon when he died. This is such a gross word, in fact, that this is the only time it is found in the entire Hebrew Bible. There are no related forms in other Semitic languages. Unfortunately, that also gives prudish English translators some wiggle room to avoid translating it, which is why your Bible, no matter the translation, probably does not say that Eglon took one final dump when he died. Some English versions simply leave it out. Others bend the meaning so that it refers to Ehud going out to another part of the palace after murdering Eglon. But the story leaves no doubt that it means that Eglon pooped on himself, which is a normal response to sudden trauma like having a guy stuff a knife into your blubber. In many English versions of the Bible, this word is daintily translated as "dirt," but the most honest translation is "crap." That's how it's rendered in the ancient Aramaic and Latin translations, and that's the translation that makes the most sense in light of the gory details of the story.

But there is one more mystery to this drama. How was Ehud able to leave the crime scene and get away scot-free? Did he waltz out of the palace, past the hapless bodyguards without even disturbing their pinochle game? Or did he have another escape route? (Cue the dramatic music.) The answer revolves around another word that is difficult to translate.

Leaving Through the Men's Room

Baruch Halpern, a professor at Pennsylvania State University, thinks architecture is the key to solving what he dubs the "oldest locked-room murder" in literature. Halpern, like a Hebrew-literate detective with too much time on his hands, has pored over the various parts

of Eglon's palace and plotted out Ehud's movements from the time
he entered to the moment he slipped away.[2] The spare account in
Judges 3 provides little architectural detail, so Halpern relies on
palaces excavated in other parts of the ancient Near East—like
Megiddo in Israel, Tell Halaf in Syria, and Tell Tayanat in Turkey—
to understand the layout of Eglon's royal residence.

Halpern says that Ehud first met Eglon in an audience hall, a
large area where the king officially received visitors. When the
king dismissed his servants so he might hear Ehud's "secret message" (which turned out to be a squelching knife to the belly), they
probably retreated to a porticoed antechamber separated from the
audience hall by doors that they would have closed behind them. (If
there are any ancient Hebrew language geeks out there, the word
for this room is *aliyya*, which describes a chamber on the upper level
of a structure.) The text tells us that Ehud "came to" Eglon while
he sat in this upper-level chamber,[3] probably climbing a set of stairs
from the audience hall to the king's throne. Once Ehud killed Eglon
and the fat king evacuated his bowels, Ehud locked the doors to the
upper room and exited via the *misdaron*.

Now things get interesting. This word *misdaron* is only found
here in the entire Bible. It is a key piece of evidence for us to figure
out how Ehud escaped without detection. Add to it another puzzle
piece, which is a word translated in many versions as "cool." It is
used twice to describe the king's upper room.[4] But Halpern points
out, and we agree, that in the hot climate of Jericho, where the story
takes place, the upper part of a building is the hottest part. For this
reason, he proposes the alternative reading of "beams," based on
the word's meaning in Psalm 104 (this is how Bible detective work
moves forward). This tells us, then, that the king's throne room was
an upper room supported by beams. Picture that: an upper room

suspended above wooden beams. Now we're coming closer to figuring out what the *misdaron* was through which Ehud escaped the crime scene.

Modern English versions of the Bible typically translate *misdaron* as "porch" or "vestibule," but there is no linguistic support for this. Just because you want it to say something nice like "porch" doesn't mean it does. Halpern thinks it more likely that *misdaron* refers to a latrine or toilet. He notes that indoor plumbing and toilets were commonly found in royal palaces from the mid-second millennium BCE on—well before the time period in which the Book of Judges is set.

Also, the Semitic root on which *misdaron* is based can mean "to be blinded, puzzled," which Halpern believes can be associated with the Israelite attitude of concealment toward excrement. The same attitude is reflected in the expression "to cover one's feet." He thinks the *misdaron* is the "hidden place" under the beams that served as the depository of the king's urine and feces. We will now quote Halpern so you can get the full disgusting impact of his meaning: "The king's droppings from above could only have fallen through the floor down below. And to this nether region, under the beams, royal janitors no doubt had access."[5]

Others have suggested that Ehud left the upper room through other routes, but their arguments are not particularly persuasive. Some propose that the throne room had a back door, which might help explain the translation "porch" or "vestibule" for *misdaron*. But if such an alternative entrance had been available, we would expect the king's servants to have used it when they became concerned that something might be wrong with him inside the locked upper room. Why would they get a key to unlock a door the king had locked instead of peeking in the back door?

Others say Ehud left the upper room the same way he entered it: by taking the stairs back down to the audience hall after he locked the king in. But Halpern observes that the text doesn't support this interpretation because the expression that's used—"he closed it upon himself"—is used only to describe a door being locked from the inside. Ehud was definitely inside the throne room with Eglon's corpse when he secured the door.

There are other reasons to think Ehud left through the latrine. If he went out the back door undetected, how would the servants know that he had left and that it was time for them to return to their master? The text suggests a cause-effect relationship between his departure and their return to Eglon. "After he had gone, the servants came."[6]

In Halpern's opinion, Ehud and the courtiers probably bumped into each other soon after the king met his end. After slithering his way through the hole in the floor that functioned as the royal john, Ehud cautiously tiptoed his way through the crap-catching room underneath. He probably exited through a door under the stairs that was used by the janitors to gather his excellency's excrement. Ehud was now back in the audience hall at the foot of the stairs leading to the upper chamber. At this point, he opened the doors that led to the porticoed antechamber, where the king's attendants were waiting to be summoned. As he strolled past them, they did not suspect a thing about what had transpired in the few moments since they saw their master alive for the last time. They returned to the audience hall. As the odor of the king's final bowel movement wafted through the air and Eglon didn't appear, they became concerned. Bounding up the stairs and fumbling with the key, they finally opened the door to the king's *en suite* quarters to discover a gruesome sight. "'Behold! There was their lord fallen dead on the floor' (verse 25), with his load dropped beside him. No blood; dagger enveloped; no sign of fiddling with the lock."[7] Israel: 1. Moab: 0.

The story of Eglon and Ehud, aka "Fatty" and "Lefty," is unique. Ehud's escape through the royal toilet adds the final deliciously repulsive touch to a story already rife with vomit-worthy images. Of course, since the Bible leaves so many details unstated, any attempt to say precisely what happened is speculative. But as Bible scholars, we find Halpern's explanation fairly convincing. It clears up lingering questions about the story that would otherwise remain unanswered.

And as guys who appreciate an occasional diversion into the disgusting, we think this makes one heck of a story.

—◦◦◦—

8

Was Onan a Jerk?

FOR CENTURIES, a guy named Onan has gotten a bad rap as the only man in the Bible to be on record as having masturbated. Prudish Christians created a euphemism for masturbation based on his name: onanism. The example of Onan, and his ultimate fate, has been used for centuries to discourage young people from taking sexual matters into their own hands, so to speak.

But was Onan really a jerk? Or was he, rather, a model of sexual control? A pioneer of population control? The first human in recorded history to use the withdrawal method? Let's take another walk on the seamy side of Bible history to find out.

Coitus Onanterruptus

Onan's story appears in Genesis 38, smack in the middle of the story of Joseph, and it seems dreadfully out of place there—like a naughty interruption of an otherwise seamless narrative. You could remove chapter 38, which tells the Onan story, and smush chapters 37 and

39 together, and they would flow together without skipping a beat. For this reason, scholars have often proposed that Onan's story was inserted, rather clumsily, into the Joseph tale, almost like a gratuitous sex scene thrust into an action movie. While it may be true that this story is an insertion (of more than one type, as we'll see), there is a certain logic to telling it in Genesis 38. The story takes place in Canaan before Jacob's family all moved to Egypt. It also depicts Joseph's older brother, Judah, as a grown man with newly married sons of his own. The supposed interruption may be the author's way of relating two simultaneous events, like saying, "Meanwhile, back in Canaan. . . ."

Onan was one of Judah's three sons. The others were Er and Shelah. We don't know why Judah named his kids after grunting and sneezing noises. Maybe he wasn't very creative. At the appropriate time, Judah found a wife for his oldest son, Er, a woman named Tamar. The Bible tells us that Er was wicked. In fact, his name actually resembles the word for wicked in Hebrew. Er erred, you might say, and God killed him. God was pretty much the judge and the jury in the Middle East back then. So Judah approached his next son, Onan, and told him, "Go in to your brother's wife and perform the duty of a brother-in-law to her; raise up offspring for your brother."[1] What he meant was, "I don't care if you find Tamar to be pleasant, attractive, or a good squeeze—bag her." The text goes on to say that Onan knew that any children he fathered by Tamar would not be his, so he refused. But he did it in a sneaky way.

Onan's secret goal was to turn each of his sexual encounters with Tamar into Mission Unaccomplished. He didn't want to give her full bang for her buck. The NRSV puts it graphically, though not very romantically, when it says, "he spilled his semen on the ground."[2] It makes you wish romance novelists had translated the Bible rather than artless language scholars. In any case, the verb in this sentence literally means "to spoil." That's exactly what happens to semen that is spilled on the ground. And Onan's semen hit the ground "whenever" he "went in to" or "joined" with Tamar. The clear sense of the Hebrew is that this happened a lot—Onan apparently didn't mind coming for the party, he just didn't want to bring a gift.

Onan's repeated coitus interruptus displeased God, who killed him as he had his older brother Er. Two of the Grunt Brothers were now wiped off the map.

The Moral of the Story: Always Pay Cash

If you're wondering what happened to poor Tamar, the story tells us and gets even more salacious. Judah's third son, Shelah, was too young to be married at the time. At least that's what Judah told Tamar. He promised that when Shelah grew up, he would marry Tamar. In the meantime, Judah sent her back home to live with her father. The story says that Judah was afraid that Shelah would die.[3] It's not clear what this means. Perhaps Shelah had a bad habit of spilling his own semen on the ground, or maybe he was doing whatever older brother Er had done to make God angry. But as the story unfolds, it appears that Judah was afraid that Tamar was cursed or had bad luck and would lead Shelah to his death as she had his previous sons. In the meantime, Tamar must have been wondering, "What's a girl got to do to get pregnant around here?"

A long time passed. Judah's wife died. Shelah grew up. But Judah did not fulfill his promise to Tamar. Finally, with the biological clock ticking loudly in her ears, Tamar took matters into *her* own hands. She learned that Judah was going away to shear sheep. She removed the mourning clothes she had been wearing since her husband died and dressed up as a prostitute, covering her face with a veil (which isn't bad advice for prostitutes today). She sat at the entrance of the town of Enaim (which means "eyes" in Hebrew, which happened to be the only part of Tamar's face that was visible). When Judah passed by, he saw her but did not recognize her because of the veil. Thinking she was a prostitute, he inquired about the cost of a good fling. Perhaps warming up to her role as a hooker, she negotiated a price: a kid (a baby goat), which he promised to send back to her. The price was acceptable to her, but she wanted some collateral until the goat arrived. She must have heard the talk from the other prostitutes that some guys enjoyed dinner but didn't pay the bill. She asked for his personal effects—his signet ring, which he wore on a cord like a necklace, and his shepherd's staff. This would be like a business today holding your driver's license as a guarantee of payment. The signet ring was especially important because it was Judah's identification, which he would need for future transactions. Judah, perhaps not the brightest guy in the messianic line, left two of his most important personal effects with her and proceeded to have his romp.

Judah may have been stupid, but at least he was honest. When he got home he tried to pay his debt. He sent a kid back with a friend. But the friend could not find the prostitute. That's because Tamar had dropped her side career. The hours must have been lousy and the health benefits terrible. She had played prostitute for just one john—the gullible Judah. Then she had returned home and dressed again in her widow's clothing, as if nothing had ever happened. But something had happened: she had become pregnant. Judah had not spilled his seed on the ground. Within months her belly swelled, and when Judah learned she was with child, he wanted to have her burned to death since, technically, she was still betrothed to Shelah, even though Shelah wasn't really following through. It was only when she produced Judah's own personal effects—his signet and staff—that he relented, confessing, "She is more in the right than I, since I did not give her to my son Shelah."[4]

The story notes that Judah did not have sex again with Tamar. Tamar gave birth to twin boys who were the ancestors of two prominent families in Israel. Perez, the older, stood at the head of the genealogy that produced both King David and Jesus. That's correct: a child born of a father and his daughter-in-law's illicit union became an ancestor of Jesus. Just listen to that collective gasp from Baptists who never learned this in their midweek Bible studies.

Stimulating Ideas

Back to our central subject, which is masturbation. Why did poor Onan's name become a byword for solo sex? And was this passage really describing a man masturbating, as some Christians even today believe? What does it mean that he "spilled his seed" other than that the floor needed a good mopping?

According to Thomas W. Laqueur, a well-known cultural historian and professor at the University of California, Berkeley, the association of masturbation with the story of Onan goes back only to the eighteenth century.[5] In 1712 an English pamphlet appeared with the title *Onania; or, The Heinous Sin of Self Pollution and all its Frightful Consequences, in both SEXES Considered, with Spiritual and Physical Advice to those who have already injured themselves by this abominable practice. And seasonable Admonition to the Youth of the nation of Both SEXES.* The author was anonymous but was probably a man named

John Marten. Notice that Marten capitalized SEX twice in the title. He knew what sold books.

Marten was a "surgeon" in a day when you didn't even need an online degree to practice medicine and putting leeches all over someone's body was considered advanced treatment. He was something of a huckster but also a brilliant marketer. His pamphlet caused a, shall we say, wide sensation in England and went through multiple editions. Its main claim, which sparked alarm, was that masturbation by both males and females was a dire threat to individual health and social order. It also established "onanism" as a term for the activity. Indeed, Marten claimed that Onan's crime, for which God killed him, was "lasciviously to grope with the privities." Not so coincidentally, the cure for this misguided desire could be found in a potion available from—you guessed it—Marten himself and his sponsoring apothecary.

The consequences of the fervor that resulted from Marten's publication have lasted even to today, and not just among people who at one time or another have lasciviously groped with their privities. In addition to the endurance of the term "onanism," fervent opposition to masturbation continues in certain Christian circles. Before the eighteenth century, the phenomenon of masturbation went largely ignored by the church. This wasn't a bad posture, since masturbation is not addressed anywhere in the Bible. But the Christian mind-set changed with the publication of Marten's pamphlet. Subsequently, masturbation was viewed as a horrible and dangerous sin.

Just how influential Marten's hoax remains became apparent in a sticky sexual scandal during the administration of President Bill Clinton. No, not *that* scandal. This was an earlier one, in 1994, when Clinton asked for the resignation of the United States Surgeon

General, Joycelyn Elders. The reason, as you may remember, especially if you keep up with news about masturbation, was that in a speech at a UN conference on the AIDS crisis, she had advocated the teaching of masturbation as a way of preventing young people from sexual activity that could spread the disease. The public outcry at her remarks was so great that she was forced out of office.

The most vocal objections to Elders's comment came from conservative Protestant Christians who were worried that the promotion of masturbation might erode public morality, especially among the young, as it almost did in 1712 until Marten saved the day with his pamphlet on the SEXES. Opposition also came from Catholics who, following the teaching of Augustine, held that sex is legitimate only for the purpose of reproduction, not pleasure. This idea is explained in the *New Catholic Dictionary*'s definition of Onanism, which reads in part:

> *The theological term for the crime committed by married persons, who in the performance of the conjugal act aim to prevent conception. . . . Onanism is always a grave sin. It is a crime opposed to natural law, for it frustrates the primary purpose of matrimony, namely, the procreation of offspring.*[6]

Who's Your Daddy?

But notice that Marten's pamphlet and the *New Catholic Dictionary* represent two different interpretations of Onan's deed. Was it masturbation or was it withdrawal? Most biblical scholars would argue that it was the latter, for two reasons. First, the expression "go to" used of a man approaching a woman is a very common idiom in the

Hebrew Bible for sexual relations. It may originate not from a description of the sex act but from the idea of a man entering a woman's tent or residence to get it on with her. But whatever its origin, its use in the present story indicates that Onan's behavior occurred while he was having sex with Tamar. Instead of climaxing inside of her, he would "spill his seed" on the ground. (The famous literary critic Dorothy Parker quipped that she named her parrot Onan for the same reason.) In other words, Onan withdrew to prevent Tamar from conceiving.

The second reason for this interpretation lies in the larger context of the practice of "levirate marriage" that is assumed in this story. The word "levir" is of Latin derivation and refers to a husband's brother. The custom of levirate marriage was found especially in certain clan societies, like ancient Israel. The way levirate marriage was supposed to work is spelled out in the Book of Deuteronomy:

> When brothers reside together, and one of them dies and has no son,
> the wife of the deceased shall not be married outside of the family
> to a stranger. Her husband's brother shall go in to her, taking her in
> marriage, and performing the duty of a husband's brother to her. And
> the firstborn whom she bears shall succeed to the name of the deceased
> brother, so that his name may not be blotted out of Israel.[7]

This was why Judah ordered Onan to "perform the duty of a brother-in-law" to Tamar.[8] Levirate marriage had several purposes. It kept a man's lineage from dying out. It also kept property within a clan or family so that it did not revert to outsiders by inheritance. This explains why Onan refused to fulfill his duty. He was selfish. He did not want *his* son to be considered his brother's. He may also have been trying to gain Er's inheritance. If Onan fathered a child by

Tamar, that child would inherit Er's property. But if Er had no son, his property might go to Onan.

Now, some interpreters recognize the levirate marriage background of this story but still contend that in "wasting his seed" Onan was gratifying himself sexually and that God killed him for this, not for refusing to reproduce. As support for this view, they point out that the punishment prescribed for failure to carry out the duty of the brother-in-law was much less severe than death. That law commanded that the widow in such a case go to the city elders and lodge a complaint. The elders were to summon the brother-in-law. If he refused in public to comply, the widow was to remove his sandal, spit in his face, and say, "This is what is done to the man who does not build up his brother's house," which would then be his reputation in Israel.[9]

But there is another dimension of this story that needs to be considered— Tamar's position in society. Another purpose of levirate marriage was the social function of making sure widows were cared for when they had no other form of sustenance. Tamar was caught in limbo. In that society, betrothal was effectively marriage that had not been consummated. Tamar was betrothed to Shelah, so she could not marry another man. But Judah obviously had no intention of allowing Shelah to marry her. She was not, apparently, in any danger of starving or becoming destitute. But living childless in her own father's house for the rest of her life was not a satisfying prospect. A woman's worth in that society was judged particularly by her success at bearing children. Onan's treatment of her was degrading. Then to isolate her, as Judah had done, was humiliating and robbed her of her life's purpose.

Tamar's solution to her dilemma—dressing as a prostitute to seduce her father-in-law—may strike us modern readers as extreme.

And in a sense, it was extreme. But it was an extreme to which Tamar was driven to preserve her own dignity and self-worth. Nowhere in the Bible is her act condemned. In fact, she appears in the genealogies of David and Jesus.[10] Matthew's version includes five women, which in itself is unusual in an Israelite genealogy. Tamar is the first of the five. The others are Rahab, Ruth, Bathsheba—who is called the "wife of Uriah"—and Mary. Each of these women had a checkered reputation: Rahab was a prostitute; Ruth spent the night with Boaz before they were married; Bathsheba had sex with David while she was married to someone else; and Mary got pregnant with Jesus before she was married to Joseph. Yet Rahab is held up as an example of great faith, a woman who believed in Israel's God and aided the spies in the conquest of Canaan. Ruth is presented as a model of love and loyalty. Bathsheba is cast as the innocent victim of David's lust and the mother of the supremely wise King Solomon. Mary is a paragon of faith and trust, specially chosen to be the mother of Jesus. Tamar fits well in this list as a woman of courage who took great risks in a time of crisis to preserve her dignity and continue her husband's line.

Seen in this light, perhaps Onan's sin had less to do with self-gratification than it did with trying to deprive another person of fulfillment and purpose. Does the Bible speak about masturbation? In our opinion, clearly not. You might say the Bible turns a blind eye to the subject.

9

What Was Isaac Doing When Rebekah First Saw Him?

M OST PEOPLE REMEMBER the precise moment they first laid eyes on the love of their life. Perhaps they saw each other across a crowded cafe or on a dance floor. Perhaps a friend introduced them at a party, or maybe they were in the same bowling league (Steve's suggestion).

But few of us first saw our lover while he or she was using the latrine. Yet that's precisely what may have happened to Rebekah, the wife of Isaac.

Stop the Camel, That's My Husband

The mystery resides in a particular word in the story of how Rebekah met Isaac. Isaac's dad, Abraham, had sent his servant to get Isaac a wife from among Abraham's own relatives who lived far away. Like some families of today, Abraham didn't want his son marrying outside "his people." And since Abraham was living among Canaanites, there weren't a lot of local Hebrew women hanging around. The servant took a long journey and had great success. He found a woman he believed was God's choice for Isaac. Her name was Rebekah, and according to the Bible account, she was a peach. She offered to water his camels, which was a lot of work considering how much camels can drink. And just like Abraham, she took a gigantic leap of faith, leaving her home and family behind to go where she believed God was directing her. She was also Isaac's cousin. Guess it ran in the family. The servant brought her back to Abraham, and while the caravan was approaching, Rebekah saw her soon-to-be husband, Isaac, for the first time. He was doing something in the field.

What exactly Isaac was doing in the field is not known because the meaning of the verb used here is uncertain. The NRSV translates it as "to walk." But careful readers will notice a footnote in their Bible stating, "Meaning of Hebrew word is uncertain." You can say that again. The meaning of the word is in fact so uncertain that at least thirteen different interpretations of it have been proposed by scholars. One scholar, Gregory Vall, who teaches at Ave Maria University in Florida, wrote an article discussing most of the interpretations.[1]

The first four possibilities all propose that the root of this verb means "talk, complain, muse." One of these suggests that Isaac was talking with someone, perhaps a friend. But the Bible does not mention anyone else being in the field with him, so this interpretation strikes us as unlikely.

Other scholars propose that Isaac was musing or meditating. This is a popular interpretation for modern translations such as the Revised Standard Version and the New International Version. But if this is the meaning of our mystery verb, then what is its point in the context of the story? Why did the author include it? What was Isaac meditating about? Vall points out another weakness: when the verb means "to meditate," it is always accompanied by the preposition "on" to explain what the person was meditating on. In this case, Isaac would have been meditating on the field, which makes no sense.

A third interpretation takes the meditation option a step further and suggests that Isaac was praying. This is the way Martin Luther translated the word. The main problem with this is that Hebrew has a perfectly good word for "pray" that you would expect the writer to use if that was what Isaac was doing. This interpretation also does not explain why Isaac went into the field, unless he was sick of being with his family back in the tents. He was, after all, forty years old and had never been married. Perhaps he was becoming the butt of jokes. And unless he practiced onanism, he was probably pretty frustrated too.

Some say Isaac was "complaining" in the sense of "lament" or "mourn," and this is the option Vall prefers. But this interpretation faces the same problem as "meditate." Hebrew has other verbs for "lament" and "cry, weep" that you would expect to find here if that was what Isaac was doing. In fact, the word they propose does not really mean "lament" but rather "complain," in the sense of expressing unhappiness or discontent. Vall, perhaps romantically, likes this option because it explains how Rebekah brought Isaac comfort after his mother's death. His "complaint" expressed deep discontent out of loneliness. It is a nice sentiment, but it still does not account for Isaac's presence in the field. He could have complained to God anywhere.

Several other interpretations suggest that this verb means to "sink down," meaning that Isaac was "low" in the sense of being depressed or sad. But the root is used in this sense only when it describes a person's inner self—a person's soul, spirit, or mood being low or depressed. The text here would have to mean that Isaac himself went into the field to physically sink down. Again, this doesn't make any sense.

Others suggest that Isaac physically lay down. Once again, Hebrew has a much more common verb that means "to lie down," and you would expect to find it here if that is what Isaac did. Besides, it is uncertain whether the root "sink" really can mean "lie down." On top of that, if Isaac was lying down, how could he have seen Rebekah's caravan coming, and how could she have seen him?

Because there is a noun from this same root that means a "hole," it has even been proposed that Isaac went into the field to dig a hole, which perhaps was a euphemism for defecating. While this interpretation explains why Isaac had to go into the field, Vall observes several problems with it. There are good Hebrew verbs meaning "dig" that you would expect to find here instead of this obscure one. There is also a good Hebrew euphemism for defecation, "to cover the feet," which occurs elsewhere in the Bible, as we have seen. Finally, the Hebrew noun meaning "hole" refers not to a small hole but to a pit, which would have been much larger than Isaac needed to dig to relieve himself, unless he'd consumed an inhumanly large amount of food.

Other interpretations rely on dubious propositions or pure guesswork. They include the idea that Isaac went out "to gather brushwood," to take a stroll, even to "walk about swinging his arms." Each of these proposes that the author used an obscure verb that is not found anywhere else in Hebrew. Sometimes there is even a common Hebrew word with the same meaning that the author could have used but didn't. Most of these ideas can't be taken seriously, but they do illustrate the lengths to which scholars have gone trying to explain our mystery verb.

Our Pick

Vall actually missed one important interpretation put forward by Gary Rendsburg, a professor at Rutgers University.[2] Rendsburg proposes a word similar in meaning to "dig a hole." He does not, however, think that it is a euphemism. Rather, he compares it to a root found in Arabic and other Semitic languages that has the sense "excrete, urinate, defecate."

Why even consider this possibility, except for the fact that it's gross and funny? It has several things going for it—chiefly, that it is used elsewhere in the Bible with this same meaning. One of these occurrences is in the Book of Isaiah.[3] The prophet Isaiah, speaking for God, expresses great anger against his people and describes a time when God caused the corpses of the people to be like excrement (NRSV "refuse") in the streets. The root is the same as that of our mystery word, though it is spelled slightly differently.

Another example is in a Proverb that discusses the ill effects of drunkenness, such as quarrels, woes, unexplained wounds, and bleary eyes.[4] In the list, a form of our mystery word pops up too. It is sometimes translated "complaint." And this translation, though vague and bland, is certainly possible. However, one of the obvious effects of drinking too much wine is frequent urination, so Rendsburg's interpretation fits particularly well with the point of the passage.

The best example of this Hebrew root referring to bodily functions is in the famous story about the prophet Elijah engaging the priests of the Canaanite god, Baal, in a test to prove whether Baal or Yahweh was the true God.[5] Each side placed a sacrifice on an altar. The worshipers then called upon their respective deities to send fire from heaven to burn up the sacrifice. Elijah eventually won the contest because Yahweh responded when he prayed, while the priests of Baal failed to summon fire from heaven. But during the contest, the mystery word is used. The priests of Baal had spent the entire morning praying to Baal. At noon Elijah started to make fun of them. He told them to cry louder because Baal was otherwise occupied. Elijah suggested that Baal was taking a trip or sleeping or going to the bathroom. The last option is an expression that contains our word. Its interpretation has also been debated, and "meditating" has been suggested for it. But in light of the way Elijah was ridiculing the priests of Baal, it almost certainly means "defecating" or "urinating."

We like Rendsburg's proposal, though it has one significant disadvantage: it doesn't speak to the idea that Isaac was comforted after his mother's death by marrying Rebekah. For that reason, and perhaps from simple revulsion, some readers may prefer to understand the mystery verb as "complain" or "meditate," as their Bible probably states. Fine. But it's still possible that Isaac was answering nature's call in the field when Rebekah first laid eyes on her dreamboat.

10

Did God Hit Jacob Below the Belt?

Genesis 32 tells the story of a weird wrestling match between Jacob and somebody—or something. Jacob was on his way back home to Canaan, which he had left over twenty years earlier. He was traveling with his four wives, eleven sons (Benjamin wasn't born yet), and one daughter. It sounds like one of those early Mormon caravans, and like the Mormons, Jacob was fleeing persecution. He had just learned that his brother Esau, whose death threats caused Jacob to leave Canaan in the first place, was coming toward him with four hundred men. In an apparent effort to protect his family, Jacob had placed his wives and children on one side of the River Jabbok and had crossed to the other side to meet Esau. There, quite out of the blue, a "man" attacked Jacob and wrestled with him all night.

The "man" was actually a supernatural being of some sort. We know this because he changed Jacob's name to Israel, which means "he wrestles with God." Also, Jacob named the place "Peniel," meaning "face of God," because he said he saw God face-to-face. In addition, a reference to this event in the Book of Hosea says that Jacob strove with an angel.[1] In the middle of the match, the supernatural being saw that he was not winning and hit or touched Jacob on the hollow or socket of his hip or thigh. The conclusion explains that this is why Israelites do not eat the body part that is on that socket (and Orthodox Jews still don't).

But scholars have long puzzled over what exactly this body part is. It is typically translated "sinew" or "nerve" or even "muscle." But it is uncertain just which sinew, nerve, or muscle the story refers to. One common understanding is that the organ in question is the sciatic nerve, which is the longest nerve in the human body, running from the hip to the heel. Other animals have a sciatic nerve running the length of their back legs too. A problem with this view, however, is that there is no special law anywhere else in the Hebrew Bible against eating the sciatic nerve. There is also no obvious reason why the eating of that particular nerve should be prohibited.

Family Jewels

A new proposal for which part of Jacob's body was injured in this wrestling match was put forward by S. H. Smith in 1990 in the prestigious British journal *Vetus Testamentum*.[2] Smith's article built on and expanded an earlier suggestion by Stanley Gevirtz, now deceased, who was a longtime respected professor at Hebrew Union College in Los Angeles.[3]

As you might have guessed from the general direction of this puerile handbook, Gevirtz and Smith think the mystery organ is the human wiener. Their arguments (like the arguments made in the "Adam's penis bone" chapter) spring from the fact that there is no formal word in the Hebrew Bible for "penis." Instead, the Bible uses various euphemisms. Smith argues that there are three euphemisms in the story of Jacob's wrestling match. The first is the word translated "hollow" or "socket." (We won't tell you what the Hebrew word is because it figures into another chapter and we don't want to ruin the surprise.) Smith asserts that this word is strongly related to a recognized euphemism for the penis in the Bible, and so he suggests that this word may be one as well. Heck, everything in the Bible is a euphemism for penis.

The second word is "thigh" (another Hebrew word we'll save for later), which is used with a wink and a nudge in several other biblical texts. When Abraham commissioned his most trusted servant to travel back to the land Abraham came from to search for a wife for his son Isaac, he called him in and said to him,

> Put your hand under my thigh and I will make you swear by the LORD, the God of heaven and earth, that you will not get a wife for my son from the daughters of the Canaanites, among whom I live, but will go to my country and to my kindred and get a wife for my son Isaac.[4]

The "thigh" here refers to Abraham's penis or scrotum. His servant swore to him while cupping Abe's goods. (Recall that the Latin root of the word "testify" also refers to the testicles, because in Rome men swore on their own testicles. That would make jury duty interesting, don't you think?)

Abraham wasn't the only one who made someone swear on his gonads. Later on in Genesis, Jacob did the same thing.[5] Jacob was dying and didn't want to be buried in Egypt. He made Joseph put his hand under his thigh and swear that Joseph would transport Jacob's body back to Canaan to be buried in the family tomb.

Modern readers probably find all this peculiar. None of the television crime dramas show witnesses taking the stand and swearing on their own groins to tell the whole truth and nothing but the truth. But the reasoning behind swearing on your dearest self makes good sense. Both Abraham and Jacob were near the end of their life. Like most old men, they were thinking a lot about having sex with younger women—just kidding. Rather, each was thinking about his family line, which of course led him to contemplate his family jewels. This sacred organ held a man's power to pass on his DNA. Since nobody knew about DNA in those days, it also represented the fulfillment of God's promise to make Abraham and his heirs a great nation and to give the land of Canaan to his descendants.

And for Jacob, who was perhaps less concerned about the perpetuation of his family line, since he already had many children, his testes represented his ancestry. He wanted to be taken back to the land of Canaan to be buried with his parents and grandparents in their family tomb, on their family land. Jacob wanted to spawn. Ancient peoples felt strongly attached to their family land, which was passed down through generations. Jacob did not want to be forgotten or isolated in death. He wanted to be buried in the land God had promised to him.

Smith also observes that the Hebrew expression translated "thigh" on several occasions in the Bible literally means "those who come forth from the thigh" and refers to a person's direct descendants. One of these passages gives the number of Jacob's family members who journeyed to Egypt as sixty-six, distinguishing between those who were his direct descendants ("from the thigh") and the wives of his sons, who were related to him only by marriage (from someone else's thigh).[6] A similar text at the beginning of Exodus sets the number of Jacob's direct descendants at seventy.[7] You also see this in the story of Gideon in the Book of Judges, which says that Gideon had seventy sons (not including daughters) and was the father of all of them by many different wives.[8] Gideon had one busy "thigh."

The third euphemism Smith finds in the Jacob story is rendered "sinew" or "nerve." (This is like shooting fish in a barrel.) This expression is actually two words in Hebrew: *gid hannasheh*. Both words are relatively uncommon in the Hebrew Bible. *Gid* occurs five times outside of Genesis 32 and refers to a body part in the nature of a sinew or tendon associated with the neck,[9] the body in general,[10] and the tail or legs.[11] In a footnote, however, Smith mentions an instance in later Hebrew where this word refers to the *"membrum virile,"* i.e., the penis.[12] Scholars like to put dirty words in Latin, perhaps to try to protect their reputations.

The other word, *nasheh,* occurs only here in the Hebrew Bible, so its exact meaning is uncertain. But both Smith and Gevirtz suggest that it may derive from the word *nefesh* ("life") or the word *enosh* ("man"), meaning "sinew of life" or "male sinew." Try that one out on your partner tonight.

Combining these three euphemisms, Smith and Gevirtz arrive at the following interpretation. In the course of the "rumble on the river," God (or God's representative) struck Jacob in the groin, causing Jacob to roll around on the ground in abject pain saying, "That's not fair!" (we surmise). At the end of the story, the author says this is why the Israelites don't eat the "male-sinew" or "life-sinew," that is, the penis of animals. The law of the Hebrew Bible doesn't specifically prohibit eating the genitals, probably because it was clearly understood that this was way the heck off limits. And anyway, as we learned before, there's too much bone in animal penises to make good eating, unless you are dining on spider monkey, which is illegal and you probably should be jailed.

On All Fours

Since Smith assumes that the words for "hand" (*yad*) and "foot" (*regel*) or "feet" are two of the most common euphemisms in the Hebrew Bible, it may be helpful to look at some passages where they are generally recognized as dirty words in disguise. One of the best examples is in the Song of Solomon. It reads:

> My beloved thrust his hand (yad) into the opening,
> and my inmost being yearned for him.[13]

Whoa. Did we stumble into the Penthouse Forum? The image here is of the male lover opening the door to the female's bedroom, but the double entendre is obvious.

For the euphemistic sense of "feet," consider the following two passages from the Book of Isaiah:

> In the year that King Uzziah died, I saw the Lord sitting on a throne high and lofty; and the hem of his robe filled the temple. Seraphs were in attendance above him; each had six wings: with two they covered their faces, and with two they covered their feet, and with two they flew.[14]

> On that day the Lord will shave with a razor hired beyond the River— with the king of Assyria—the head and the hair of the feet, and it will take off the beard as well.[15]

The first passage describes a vision of God that the prophet Isaiah had in the temple. The creatures attending God, called Seraphs ("burning ones"), were apparently something like angels with three pairs of wings. They flew with one pair, covered their faces with one pair, and covered their feet with the third pair. The latter two actions were signs of reverence in God's presence. Some have interpreted "feet" to mean the literal appendages and have pointed to the story of Moses removing his sandals in God's presence.[16] But the comparison doesn't really work, because Moses was exposing his feet rather than covering them. There is no precedent in the Bible—or elsewhere so far as we know—for anyone covering their feet as a sign of reverence or humility. But interpreting "feet" as a euphemism for the genitals makes perfect sense in view of the sense of modesty commonly associated with those organs.

The euphemistic use of "feet" is even more evident in the quote from Isaiah 7. Here, the prophet was threatening the destruction of the nation of Judah at the hands of an invading army from Assyria. The king of Assyria is likened to a razor that will "shave" the countryside of Judah, leaving it barren and empty. The land, therefore, is compared to a man's body. The specific areas to be shaved are the head, beard, and feet. Shaving the head and beard, of course, is perfectly understandable. But the only way to make sense of shaving the feet (unless you're a Hobbit) is to recognize that the word is a euphemism for the pubic region.

There's even one instance of a *double* double entendre—two euphemisms in one. This is in 1 Kings 12, where the northern tribes of Israel came to Rehoboam to approve him as their king. They asked him, though, to lighten the tax and labor burden that his father, Solomon, imposed on them. He responded by telling them that he would be tougher than his father, and he chose a crude way of putting it. "My little finger is thicker than my father's loins," he said.[17] The loins, by definition, are the seat of the reproductive organs and can be used to refer specifically to them. What is most interesting about this sentence, however, is that the word "finger" is not in the Hebrew text. It might be translated as "my little (one)" or "my little (member)," or, even better, "my weenie." In the same context with the word "loins," it is a euphemism for the penis. Rehoboam is boasting that his penis is thicker than his father's whole torso. We assume he was exaggerating.

Equal Opportunity Employment

The euphemisms in the Bible aren't used just for male genitals. There are some for female equipment as well. One of these is in a poem in the Song of Solomon (or Song of Songs) that describes a full frontal view of the female lover beginning with her feet and proceeding upward:

> How graceful are your feet in sandals,
>   O queenly maiden!
> Your rounded thighs are like jewels,
>   the work of a master hand.
> Your navel is a rounded bowl
>   that never lacks mixed wine.
> Your belly is a heap of wheat,
>   encircled with lilies.
> Your two breasts are like two fawns,
>   twins of a gazelle.
> Your neck is like an ivory tower.
> Your eyes are like pools in Heshbon,
>   by the gates of Bath-rabbim.
> Your nose is like a tower of Lebanon,
>   overlooking Damascus.
> Your head crowns you like Carmel,
>   and your flowing locks are like purple.[18]

The translation "thighs" here doesn't fit very well. The poem compares the thighs to jewels. The Hebrew word translated as "jewels" is used only one other time in the Hebrew Bible, where it is paralleled with a ring of gold.[19] Here the NRSV translates the word as "ornament." The parallel indicates that the word in question refers to a small "jewel" or "ornament"—about the size of a ring—rather than something the size of a thigh. The ornament in the second passage is also made of gold, like the ring.

The comparison with jewels seems to indicate a body part other than thighs in the Song of Solomon poem. And since "thigh" is used for the reproductive organ in other passages, as we saw earlier, it may have a similar meaning in Song of Solomon. Of course, in Song of Solomon it refers to the female organs that are visible from a frontal view. This would also explain why the word in the Song of Solomon poem is in the plural. It probably refers, in other words, to the parts of the female vulva—the labia—the larger labia and perhaps the smaller labia as well. These would be more the size of jewels. They are rounded, as described in Song of Solomon—especially so when a woman is sexually aroused. This interpretation fits the sexual nature of Songs of Solomon, as erotic literature, especially well.

Even though Smith missed the euphemism in Song of Solomon, he did include another female example. In another part of his article, he suggests that the story of Jacob and Esau's birth also contains a euphemism.[20] In that story as it is usually read, the twins, Esau and Jacob, wrestled in the womb. Esau was born first. Then Jacob came out second holding on to his brother's heel. Smith proposes that "heel" here was another euphemism for the male genitals. But he bases this proposal on the fact that it occurs in Jeremiah as an obvious euphemism for the female variety: "It is for the greatness of your iniquity that your skirts are lifted up and you are violated."[21]

The image is that of Jerusalem as a woman who is raped. The last expression is literally "your heels are violated," which makes little sense unless "heels" is a euphemism. After all, the skirt would hardly need to be lifted to access the literal heels. What is envisioned as violated are the opposing sides of the vulva. Similarly, Smith reasons, the single form, "heel," is a euphemism for Esau's sexual organ in Genesis 25.

As if he needed further support for his colorful reading, Smith cites the poem in Hosea 12, which he thinks brings the two wrestling episodes together:

> *In the womb he took his brother by the "heel,"*
> *And in his manhood he strove with God.*[22]

The idea, according to Smith, is that Jacob took over his brother's procreative power and therefore his right to the promise inherited from his grandfather and father, Abraham and Isaac. In the encounter at the Jabbok, however, God's striking Jacob on his privates was a way of reminding him that he owed his power and fertility not to his own strength or cleverness but to God's blessing.

Smith and Gevirtz have compiled a pretty convincing case for the existence of a number of different euphemisms in the story of Jacob's wrestling match at the Jabbok. None of the words discussed here is always or necessarily a euphemism for the sexual organs. But then, that's the beauty of euphemisms. They work both sides of the fence.

This is the point that Smith makes in discussing the overall perspective of the Jacob story. None of the euphemisms in that story is an explicit reference to the sexual organs. They are all merely suggestive. But this suggestiveness fits well with the whole story, which is focused on Jacob's role as the heir to the promises given to Abraham and Isaac, on the one hand, and as the progenitor of the nation of Israel through his twelve sons on the other. The story of Jacob is all about family, descendants, and heritage. It is all about the ancestral line that passes through Jacob's "loins," "hand," "feet," "palm," "thigh," "male sinew," "finger," and "heel"—which ultimately point to the same special place on Jacob's body.

~

11

Did King David Have
a Potty Mouth?

As MOST READERS KNOW, men and dogs love to pee when-ever and wherever they can. Modern laws usually prohibit men from whizzing in public, reflecting the strong influence of women in politics these days, but just tag along on any camping or fishing trip or pay a visit to a construction site and you'll find men unzipping at opportune moments and leaving their marks proudly upon trees, rocks, bushes, and walls—anything that happens to be in their trajectory.

Peeing comes into play in one of the most artfully told stories in the Bible—that of David and Abigail.[1] This story takes place against a background of serious strife between David and King Saul. Saul had become jealous and fearful of David's success, so Saul tried nu-merous times to kill him. David fled into the wilderness, where he surrounded himself with a small army that survived by making raids on foreign villages and undoubtedly peeing on their bushes, trees, and walls too. That's one privilege of belonging to a small army.

A Fool and His Money

Our story gets rolling with a man named Nabal who lived in the town of Carmel in the Judean wilderness. Nabal was very wealthy, but he had a nasty personality. As the NRSV puts it, he was "surly and mean."[2] In fact, the name "Nabal" means "fool." But Nabal's wife was his opposite in character. Her name was Abigail, and she is described as "clever and beautiful." How they ended up together, nobody knows. Maybe it was one of those unexpected high school matches—the smart girl marrying the stoner, say. Or perhaps she thought she could change him. Come to think of it, not much has changed in several thousand years.

Back at the ranch—Nabal's ranch—it was sheep-shearing time, which meant great celebration. Who doesn't like a full slate of sheep-related festivities? During this high time, Nabal received an envoy from David. Perhaps David was hoping to catch Nabal in a generous mood, swept up in the élan of wool gathering. David's envoy consisted of ten men, and they brought a request for provisions. They needed food. In his message, David pointed out how he and his men had protected Nabal's shepherds and sheep in their wilderness pastures. The request, perhaps familiar to anyone who's been threatened by the local mafia, may have felt like a shakedown to Nabal. But at least it was polite.

Nabal's response was neither polite nor smart. He insulted David, calling him a runaway slave and a vagabond. Perhaps the wool fibers had gone to Nabal's brain. Or perhaps he felt that particular bravado people often feel when surrounded by skinny, quivering sheep. Predictably, his response infuriated David, who gave orders for his men to put on their swords and march against Nabal. Meanwhile, one of Nabal's servants, sensing the danger they were in, called upon Abigail and explained the situation to her. She hurried to load provisions on donkeys and rode off to intercept David before he could kill her husband.

As she approached him, David was swearing to avenge the insult he had suffered from Nabal by killing every man in his household. Abigail dismounted her donkey and bowed down to the ground in front of him. She apologized for her husband and offered David the provisions she had brought. Speaking with great eloquence and not a little flattery, she argued that it was in David's own best interests not to carry out his murderous threats against Nabal. She expressed her confidence that God would make David king. But, she continued, if David killed all of Nabal's men, many innocents would die, and their blood would be a stain on David's reputation and an obstacle to his future kingship. Abigail ended her speech with a veiled proposal of marriage, asking him to remember her "when Yahweh has dealt well with my lord." Abigail's method of approaching David was so smooth that it seems to us that she had probably saved Nabal's bacon before when other business relationships had gone sour, but that is neither here nor there.

Abigail returned home to find Nabal drunk, so happy was he with the success of sheep-shearing season. She wisely waited until the next morning to tell him what she had done, perhaps to avoid being hurt in a drunken fit of rage. When she told him what she had done, "his heart died within him; he became like a stone." Ten days later, he gave up the ghost. Shortly thereafter, David sent for Abigail and married her. He knew a good woman when he saw one.

%&#+@ ^*!

Now back to our original subject: public urination. Buried in this story is a choice vulgarity uttered by David, the man after God's own heart, that relates to this most male of activities. We turn to the work of Peter J. Leithart, a theologian and pastor, who points out that the expression David used for "male" in this passage literally means "one who pisseth on the wall."[3] He is not making this up. Grab the King James Bible you inherited from your grandmother, dust it off, and look up 1 Samuel 25:22. Yes, the Bible says, "pisseth," in a wonderful collision of playground crudity and hifalutin English.

Leithart suggests that David used vulgar language as a kind of locker-room pep talk to drive home his point about Nabal's insult to him and his men.[4] But Leithart also asserts that this lowbrow expression is more than a stand-alone statement. It ties into several features of the story. Thus, at the beginning of the story, Nabal is called a "Calebite," a name nearly identical in Hebrew to the word for "dog." Dogs are well known for urinating on walls and anything else with a vertical profile, and they have the great fortune of not being constrained by law from doing so. David and his men are likened to a protective wall around Nabal's shepherds.[5] The idea is that Nabal was like a dog, pissing on the protection that David and his men had provided in the wilderness. Them's fightin' words.

To add to this image, Nabal's name is very similar to the word for "bottle" or "wineskin" (nebel), and he is portrayed as having been filled with wine. In fact, Leithart argues, the expression usually translated "when the wine had gone out"[6] should be rendered "while the wine was going out." He believes, in other words, that Abigail told her husband about her meeting with David while Nabal was seeing a man about a horse. For you non-Texans, that means he was taking a leak, full as he was from wine he had drunk the night before. Again, Abigail showed real smarts: if Nabal had become angry at her for meeting with David, she would have had a head start while he finished shaking the dew off his lily. In the overall scheme of the story, this element fits nicely with the meaning of David's vulgarity.

Piss-Poor Analysis?

Does Leithart's pissy proposal work? Yes, with two minor adjustments. The first is to point out (because we are nitpicky Bible experts) that the word for "wall" in the phrase "one who pisses on the wall" is not the same as the one used by Nabal's servant in referring to David and his men (verse 16). Both words, however, do denote a similar structure, so they might conjure up the same idea in the minds of readers. We'll give that one to you, Leithart.

Second, the time reference in verse 37 is not quite as certain as Leithart claims. The grammatical construction there usually denotes simultaneous action. But it does not have to be translated "while." It could just as accurately be rendered "as soon as," "when," or "after" the wine went out of him. What we're trying to say is that Nabal might have been whizzing or he might have just finished whizzing. In either case, Leithart is right that the expression refers literally to the wine leaving Nabal. This implication is often missed in translations that go for the G-rating and simply say something to the effect that Nabal had sobered up.

Leithart is also right about the literal meaning of the phrase for "male" being "one who pisses on the wall," as you can plainly see in the King James Bible. This may seem crude to us today, but it may not have been in previous times and cultures. The King James Bible, which was a model of proper English at the time it was produced, clearly shows that what is considered vulgar or inappropriate language may change over time. The verb "to piss" was considered polite social talk in sixteenth-century England but is now regarded as profane. We don't know what Hebrew expressions the ancient Israelites might have considered profane or vulgar—none of their Dictionaries of Bad Words have survived. David's expression may have been intended to rile up his troops. Or he may have simply been stressing his intention to kill all the *males*. That left only Abigail, a female, to avert disaster. Still, it is a safe bet that the image of someone urinating on you would be as unwelcome then as it is today. So we buy Leithart's suggestion that David was alluding to Nabal as a dog urinating on the "wall" of David and his men.

Leithart is also on target in noting the literary sophistication of this story. Its eloquent narration highlights the importance of the episode. With David's marriage to Abigail, he gained wealth and prominence among the Calebites that had belonged to Nabal. Since the Calebites were the leading clan in Judah, it was not long before David moved up to become king over Judah and from there to the throne of all Israel. The episode of the death of Nabal and his marriage to Abigail was more than a pit stop for David—it marked a watershed moment in his career.

12

Does the Bible Command Bikini Waxing?

T HE LAST PLACE you might expect to find a divine dictate for pubic shaving is in the last four books of the Pentateuch. These books are considered so dry and tedious that even evangelicals, known for their biblical devotion, rarely make it through alive. Viewed as a vast wasteland of verbal tedium, akin to reading the federal penal code, the books contain long lists of laws God gave to Moses soon after the Israelites escaped from Egypt and began their forty-year sightseeing tour of the desert. The most famous regulations found here are the Ten Commandments. But among the litany of rules are some hidden gems, and this chapter takes up an especially good one.

First, a quick legal lesson for your own good. The Israelite codes in the Pentateuch included two types of laws—those that supplied punishments and those that didn't. The Ten Commandments are an example of the second kind: they did not come with a punishment. But many other Hebrew laws did. For example, here's a colorful one you don't see practiced much anymore except maybe in Saudi Arabia: "When the daughter of a priest profanes herself through prostitution, she profanes her father; she shall be burned to death."[1]

And try these others on for size:

"Whoever curses father or mother shall be put to death"[2] *(meaning no kid today would survive).*

"You shall not permit a female sorcerer to live."[3]

"You shall not have sexual relations with any animal and defile yourself with it, nor shall any woman give herself to an animal to have sexual relations with it: it is perversion."[4]

"You shall not make any gashes in your flesh for the dead or tattoo any marks upon you: I am the LORD."[5]

The strange thing about these laws is that they indicate people must have been doing these things—getting tattoos, having sex with animals, cursing Mom and Dad, and practicing sorcery. Some "chosen people." No wonder God let all (but two) of them die in the desert.

The Problem in a Nutshell

Now let's shine our bright light of research on perhaps the strangest crime mentioned in the Bible: grabbing a man's cojones. The Scripture states:

If men get into a fight with one another, and the wife of one intervenes to rescue her husband from the grip of his opponent by reaching out and seizing his genitals, you shall cut off her hand; show no pity.[6]

This has probably happened to all of us. You get into a fight with another guy, and your wife rushes into the fray and grabs the guy's testicles to try to break it up. Ouch! These days a simple "I'm sorry" and perhaps a friendly lawsuit restores order. But in Old Testament times, such a common mistake was punishable by much more than that. In fact, this is the only law in the Hebrew Bible that demands physical mutilation as punishment. (You might interject, if you were alert enough, "What about the law that says 'an eye for an eye'?" Well, smarty-pants, that legislation, which is called the *lex talionis*, means "law of retaliation," which you probably did not know, and is more about limiting vengeance by inflicting equivalent damage on the guilty party. And anyway, it doesn't specifically prescribe mutilation.[7])

After reading this passage from Deuteronomy, the women are probably asking, "Why would the code demand the amputation of the woman's hand when all she did was give the guy's balls a firm squeeze? His pain would subside after a few minutes, but her hand would never grow back." Scholars, those overeducated, underpaid people currently teaching your children job skills, try to answer this question in several ways.

Some sadistic scholars take the text at face value. The woman's hand should be amputated because that's what she deserved, they say. These scholars tend to be men with humiliating testicle-grabbing experiences in their past. But they have one strong point: if a woman back then put a viselike grip on a man's testicles, he could lose his reproductive powers. That was a serious crime and perhaps worthy, at least in those days, of the Saudi royal hand chop.

The other way these scholars justify hand amputation is to see the crime as a really bad social faux pas. By roughing up (or even just touching) the genitals of a man who is not her husband, the woman has shamed herself, her husband, and her victim, and she must suffer the consequences. If she didn't, all the other ladies would get the idea they could go around grabbing their neighbors' nuts at a whim. Not good for social order.

But there's an interesting fact about this text that we haven't disclosed. The Hebrew uses two different terms for the word "hand." To start, the woman reaches out her *yad* (hand), but at the end of the passage her *kaf* is cut off. *Kaf* in ancient Hebrew means "hand" and sometimes refers euphemistically to a person's private parts. We'll show you how in a few minutes. Naturally scholars get little kicks out of suggesting that the punishment is actually a type of genital mutilation, perhaps clitoridectomy. (One of the first scholars to propose this was Lyle Eslinger in a 1981 article with an awesome pulp fiction–sounding title: "The Case of the Immodest Lady Wrestler in Deuteronomy 25:11–12."[8])

A shortcoming of both these alternatives is that they still see the woman's punishment as some kind of physical mutilation or maiming, which far exceeds the crime. As we mentioned before, no other crime demands mutilation as punishment.

A Slap on the Wrist

The scholar Jerome T. Walsh throws us a life preserver.[9] He points out that while in some places the word *kaf* means "hand," elsewhere in the Bible it refers to a particular part or quality of the hand. In some references, the *yad* (hand) has a *kaf* (specific part of the hand). For example, Jezebel, easily the baddest babe in the Bible, meets her fate in a gruesome and sort of funny way—several eunuchs daintily throw her out a window and she's trampled to death by horses and eaten by dogs. Talk about piling it on. When the soldiers not-so-daintily rush downstairs to retrieve her corpse, all that remains are her skull, feet, and the *kafs* of her two *yads*.[10]

What is this *kaf*? In light of usage elsewhere in the Bible, it most likely refers to the palms of Jezebel's hands. Sometimes a *kaf* refers to a bowl or spoon used in the temple's ceremonies. It can also refer to the branch of a palm tree. It describes the hollow of a sling,[11] like the one used by David to kill Goliath. The sole of the foot is also called a *kaf*.[12] All of these objects are curved or cupped. When the word *kaf* is used in reference to the hand, it usually describes grasping or holding rather than striking or pointing. So when *kaf* is used to denote part of the hand, it must mean the palm.

But how do you cut off someone's palm? Perhaps you don't. Walsh thinks *kaf* has a sexual connotation. You knew we'd take it there.

Walsh supports his theory by pointing to the wrestling match between Jacob and a mysterious unknown figure, which we discussed in chapter 10.[13] After wrestling together all night, the other combatant ends the match by touching Jacob on the *kaf-yerek*. This is typically translated as "hip joint" or "hollow of the thigh," but Walsh thinks Jacob's opponent has borrowed a tactic from the immodest lady wrestler in Deuteronomy, because the Hebrew word *yerek*, "thigh," can sometimes refer to the reproductive organs, as we saw. You may recall, for example, that two passages referring to Jacob, who must have had a *kaf-yerek* worth talking about, describe his descendants as those who come forth from his *yerek*.[14] "Hip" or "thigh" would hardly be an accurate translation here.

Even more instructive is a steamy sexual fantasy in Song of Solomon in which a hot and bothered young lady envisions a tryst with her man.[15] Using the plural form of *kaf*, she describes "myrrh" flowing over the *kafot-hamanul,* which spineless Bible translators usually render as "handles of the bolt." Right—"handles of the bolt," my foot. (Or rather, my *kaf-yerek*.) Song of Solomon is one long sex poem, thick with erotic metaphors and wordplay, which suggests strongly that this Hebrew phrase alludes to the woman's genital area, not the Masterlock on her chamber door.

This analysis of *kaf* allows Walsh to conclude that in some cases it describes "the open concave curves of the pelvic region, and would correspond most closely to the English word 'groin' or perhaps 'crotch.'"[16]

Okay, so Walsh got to use the words "groin" and "crotch" in a scholarly journal. Fine. But how do you cut off someone's groin? Remember, that's the punishment we're talking about here. Or is it? Walsh goes against all translations and commentaries, which agree that the woman's *kaf* is to be cut off. He believes they misunderstand the Hebrew verb *qatsats*—them's fighting words among Bible geeks. In Hebrew, verbs can appear in many different conjugations, each with its own impact on the verb's meaning. The basic verbal conjugation is called the *qal* form. Another common conjugation is the *piel,* which intensifies the meaning. For example, if the *qal* meaning of a verb is "to break," the *piel* meaning might be "to smash to pieces."

The root of the verb *qatsats* appears about fifteen times in the Hebrew Bible. The great majority have it in the *piel* form, which intensifies it to mean "to cut off," among other things. It's found, for example, in the Book of Judges in the description of another weird punishment: "Adoni-bezek fled; but they pursued him, and caught him, and cut off his thumbs and big toes."[17] The other times it appears in its less intense form, including in the text we're talking about here. In the Book of Jeremiah, it refers to a group of people who live in the desert and are called the *qetsutse peah*. The second word means "edge" or "side," and the phrase appears to designate a group of people who had strange haircuts on the sides of their heads (we kid you not).[18] Walsh argues that this meaning best fits the verb in Deuteronomy 25:12. He says, "It seems reasonable, then, to infer that *qatsats* (*qal*) means not 'to amputate,' but 'to cut or shave [hair],' particularly when it is used in conjunction with a term that can refer to a part of the body where hair grows."[19] He therefore concludes that the punishment for a woman who grabs the balls of a man (who is not her husband) during a fight is the removal of her pubic hair. The text he proposes is, "You shall shave [the hair of] her groin."

Why would pubic shaving be considered punishment? Many modern women shave the hair down there as part of a regular grooming routine. But in ancient Israel, shaving hair was a form of humiliation. The clearest example, according to Walsh, is in Isaiah 7:20, where God played the role of a barber who promised to use the king of Assyria as a razor to shave off all the hair of the Israelites, to embarrass and disgrace them as prisoners of war. The text distinguishes between the hair of the head and the "hair of the feet," which is a common Hebrew metaphor for genitals. (God was indeed threatening to shave their heads and their groins.) So shaving the pubic region was truly humiliating for a woman in ancient societies.

The Bare Truth

How do you like that? We went from biblical Hebrew to women shaving their pubes. This should increase our teenage readership. But who's to say Walsh isn't just pawning off a theory on us for his own amusement? Why do we even listen to this guy?

For one thing, he knows ancient Hebrew. It would be impossible to come up with this reading without being tuned in to the language's nuances. The distinction he makes between the meanings of the verb in its *qal* and *piel* conjugations is often overlooked even by the most experienced Bible scholars—us included.

His approach is also appealing because it makes the punishment fit the crime. We can almost hear Moses announcing, "Ladies, listen up. If you grab a guy's balls, even in an effort to save your husband during a fight, you're going to get shaved where the sun don't shine. Got it? Now, moving on to stolen donkeys. . . ." The offending woman's public humiliation at having her pubic hair shaved matches the offended man's shame at having some chick give him the knuckleballer. It's not "eye for an eye," but it's pretty darn close. Walsh's interpretation also resolves the problem of this being the only offense in the Bible for which physical mutilation is the penalty.

So we think the Bible may well command bikini waxing or at least pubic shaving— but as a punishment, not a beauty aid. My, how times have changed.

13

Was Jael a Dominatrix?

ONE OF OUR FAVORITE T-shirts reads, OLD GUYS RULE. That was certainly true in ancient Israel. It was a patriarchal society (old guys ruled!), and genealogies were traced through male lines. That's why most of the stories in the Bible (have you noticed?) are about men. Women usually appear in stereotypical "good" roles as wives and mothers (think June Cleaver, Harriet Nelson, or Edith Bunker if you're into vintage TV like we are) or in "bad" roles as prostitutes and temptresses (think Pamela Anderson. Okay, now stop thinking of Pamela Anderson). Women in the Bible are rarely portrayed as CEOs or political leaders, which is one reason why the Bible ain't so popular with the *Ms.* magazine set.

But there are important exceptions in the Bible to "old guys rule." One of them is the story of Jael.[1] You've probably never heard of Jael, but her story is remarkable for a couple of reasons. First, Jael and most of the people in the story except for the "bad guy" are women. It's like a Hebrew version of *Charlie's Angels*, and like Charlie's Angels, these women stepped way outside of the stereotypical roles and proved to be courageous warriors.

Also, very remarkably, there are two versions of this story in the Bible, one written in prose[2] and one written in poetry.[3] The poem is one of the oldest in the Bible, meaning that this story was an ancient and highly regarded tradition in Israel. Apparently, God's chosen people liked female action heroes as much as modern audiences do.

Jael's Tale

Jael's brief, heroic story is set in the time of the judges, the national leaders who ruled Israel before there were kings. The judge at the time was a woman named Deborah. She was also a prophet. One day Deborah received a message from God for Barak, the commander of the Israelite army. God said to attack the Canaanites, who had subjugated Israel. But Barak, either because he was a massive weenie or because he had such great confidence in Deborah's leadership, refused to go to war unless she accompanied him. Deborah agreed to go with him but warned that as a result the enemy general, Sisera, would be killed by a woman.

Sure enough, God caused Sisera's army to panic, and the Bible says that they were all killed except for Sisera, who fled on foot. He came to the tent of a woman named Jael, whom Sisera took to be a typical shrinking violet and not the femme fatale she proved to be. Jael invited him in to rest and gave him some milk to drink—the first step in her devious plan. Sisera, like a pleased kitty who'd been out all night, fell asleep. While he was sleeping, Jael took a tent peg and a hammer and drove the peg through his temple, killing him. Do we have to explain why we absolutely *love* this story?

There is even a postscript. After reporting his death, the final scene in the poem takes us back to Sisera's palace. His mother was looking anxiously through the palace window and wondering aloud why he was taking so long to return. Her ladies-in-waiting reassured her that Sisera was simply enjoying the spoils of war (or, perhaps, some warm milk and a tent peg through the head—ha ha!). That detail about "spoils" implies that Sisera's mother and her attendants thought Sisera was enjoying illicit battlefield sex with the captive Israelite women and that he would bring home the women's garments for his mother. They were right in one respect—Sisera was getting nailed, though not in the way they imagined.

If the Tent's A-Rockin'. . .

Susan Niditch, a prominent Bible scholar who teaches at Amherst College in Massachusetts, isn't so sure that Sisera got pegged through the head. Niditch sees sex everywhere she looks in this story.[4] For example, she points out that Jael came to Sisera in secret (NRSV: "went softly").[5] The expression "come to" (Hebrew ba el) occurs commonly in the Bible as an idiom for sexual intercourse. The phrase "in secret" is also found in the story of Ruth in the scene at the threshing floor, another steamy Bible moment.[6]

But the main verse on which Niditch builds her case is Judges 5:27, which states that Sisera fell dead at Jael's feet. This too has strong sexual connotations. (When you're a hammer, everything's a nail, isn't it?) Niditch points out that a more literal translation is that Sisera fell "between her legs." She further observes that in this same verse Sisera is described as "kneeling" or "bowing" (NRSV: "sank") and falling "between her legs," so that his posture was that of a would-be lover. This verse also says that Sisera "lay" at Jael's feet. This is another well-known idiom for sex in Hebrew as well as in English. Finally, Niditch notes that the last word in 5:27, translated "dead" in the NRSV, means "despoiled, devastated." She quotes Jeremiah, where the same word is used in a metaphorical description of Jerusalem as a woman who has been violated by her lovers.[7]

Niditch concludes that the language of the Jael story, especially in Judges 5:27, is deliberately ambivalent. It evokes both violent death and sex at the same time. Niditch says that this combination of sex and death is a common theme in battle epics and that the story of Jael makes sense in this light because, as women have long been aware, sex can be a way of asserting power.

Pegged

Niditch's observations about the double meanings in this story have a great deal to recommend them. In many ways—even some not noticed by Niditch—sex and female-male relations appear subtly as themes in these two chapters. For instance, the first line of the poem alludes to the prominence of women in the story and perhaps in Israelite society at the time when it says, "When locks were long in Israel."[8] That means the women, for once, were on top. The prose writer also amps up the sexual tension by saying that Jael penetrated Sisera with a peg—a phallic weapon—thus reversing sexual roles. This reversal of roles is exactly what Deborah had prophesied to Barak.

What exactly did Jael do to Sisera in the tent? Was it a bump-off—or the bump and grind? We may never know, but it's plausible that she may have bagged him in a different way than commonly thought.

14

Did Jacob Use Sex Toys?

I F YOU STILL FEEL GUILTY about making out with your cousin in fourth grade, let the Bible free you of shame. The Bible is full of kissing cousins like Isaac and Rebekah and like Jacob and Rachel and Rachel's sister, Leah. These couples did a lot more than kiss. They got married and had kids. And these kids became the twelve tribes of Israel.

Cousin marriage wasn't just for way back then, you know. Albert Einstein married his cousin and gained intimate knowledge of the theory of relativity. Charles Darwin married his first cousin and had ten children by her. Insert practically any joke about natural selection here.

But this chapter isn't just about kissing cousins; it's also about fake sheep penises. (If you have ever been involved with your cousin and fake sheep penises simultaneously, perhaps you do have something to feel guilty about.) The technical term for fake sheep penis is "animal dildo," kind of an ugly, porn-catalog word, but it's possible, at least according to one scholar, that these devices pop up in the Bible in the story of Jacob and Laban.

All in the Family

But let's start with kissing cousins. They always go better first. Cousin number one, who is also this story's bachelor number one, is Jacob. You may recall that Jacob conspired with his mother, Rebekah, to deceive his aging father, Isaac, and cheat his older twin brother, Esau, out of his rightful blessing. Esau was furious at having been cheated and vowed to kill Jacob. So Rebekah sent Jacob, her favorite son, away (catch the rerun in Genesis 27).

This Semitic soap opera continued as Jacob fled to Uncle Laban's house. Jacob was supposed to find safe haven there until Esau cooled down. Laban welcomed Jacob with open arms—at first. Fish and visitors smell in three days, and after a month Jacob smelled like an abandoned cannery. So Laban did what most annoyed hosts do. He told Jacob, "Because you are my kinsman, should you therefore serve me for nothing? Tell me, what shall your wages be?"[1] This was a not-so-polite way of telling Jacob that his stint as a guest was over and it was time to quit hanging around the living room playing PlayStation and drinking more than his fair share of Cokes. It was time for Jacob to earn his keep. But in the meantime Jacob had fallen for—you guessed it—his cousin Rachel. He actually fell in love with her when he first saw her shepherding her father's sheep,[2] which apparently was a major turn-on to single guys back then.

Jacob wanted to marry Rachel, but having fled from his home with little more than the clothes on his back, he had nothing to offer as a bride price except for his labor. So he offered to work for Laban for seven years in exchange for Rachel's hand. Laban, who wasn't studied up on the genetic sciences and therefore had nothing against cousin marriage, agreed to the terms. In fact, cousin marriage was common in ancient tribal societies. They preferred to have slightly odd-looking children rather than mingle their blood with other tribes. Isn't life such a balancing act?

But now the story of the would-be kissing cousins gets complicated and potentially weird. Jacob lived up to his end of the bargain. In fact, the seven years "seemed to him but a few days because of the love he had for her."[3] Sweet guy, huh? When that seven years ended, Jacob was more than ready for his bride. He told Laban, and we quote, "Give me my wife that I may go in to her."[4] That's a fairly blunt thing to say to your future father-in-law. It basically means, "After seven years I'm as horny as a goat. Give me your daughter or I will explode."

But Laban pulled a fast one. He secretly gave Jacob his older, evidently less attractive daughter, Leah, whose name means (let's all enjoy this together now) "wild cow." Jacob went through the wedding ceremony with Leah, said "I do," and poured out seven years of pent-up desire on her before discovering that he'd porked the wrong pie. It was the next morning when, after sleeping off the effects of the heavy partying he'd done at the reception, he woke up and noticed the switcheroo. The Bible describes the situation simply and elegantly: "When the morning came . . . it was Leah!"[5] Bang. Suddenly, Jacob found himself hitched to the family's wild cow. But what could he do? He was far away from home. He owned nothing that Laban hadn't given him. He had nothing to bargain with. As Leah lay there smiling at him (we surmise), he leaped out of bed, wrapped a sheet around his waist, and ran off to find Laban, who must have been getting a huge kick out of the whole situation. But when Jacob confronted him, Laban defended the deception by citing a local custom: as the older daughter, Leah had to get married before Rachel. Laban may have been making this up, hiding behind "local customs" the way small-town cops in the South use phony local statutes to force innocent motorists to pay exorbitant fines for breaking laws that don't really exist, thereby ruining family vacations (that was Steve—he's a little bitter about something). But Laban had won this round and successfully dealt his Old Maid to Jacob. No longer would she mope around Laban's house complaining that nobody would date her.

There was one upside for Jacob, but it came at a price. Laban offered to give Rachel to Jacob in marriage a week later if Jacob agreed to work for him another seven years. Smitten by Rachel, and perhaps digging the idea of sleeping with sisters, Jacob accepted the new terms, married Rachel, and put in another seven-year shift for Laban.

We promise we're almost to the part about fake sheep penises.

When the second seven years ended, Jacob told "Dad" (Laban) that he wanted to take his cousin-wives and children and leave. He was determined to get out of Dodge. But God had blessed the fruit of Jacob's labor, and Laban had prospered from it. He didn't want his star employee to go and asked him, in effect, what it would take to get him to stay. A bigger bonus? Matching 401(k) contributions? More entrée choices in the cafeteria? But Jacob wanted none of it. He asked Laban to pony up his back wages and proposed that for his wages he would go through Laban's flock and pick out the speckled and spotted sheep and goats and the black lambs. Laban would keep the rest. Laban agreed, but had a final trick up his cloak. Later that day, he went through his flock and removed the sheep and goats that had markings on them, along with the black lambs, and had these animals taken far away so that Jacob would not find them. When Jacob got around to reviewing Laban's flock, he would have to leave empty-handed.

Weird Science

This time, though, Jacob fought fire with fire. According to the usual interpretation of this story, Jacob took fresh wooden poles and stripped off their bark, creating stripes and blotches on them. Then he set these poles in front of the watering troughs where the sheep mated. He did this particularly in front of the stronger animals, so that Laban's flocks, especially the healthier specimens, produced spotted, speckled, and striped offspring, which in turn became Jacob's property. As a result, Jacob grew rich, while Laban's livestock diminished. So justice was finally served on one of the Old Testament's most conniving tricksters.

Jacob's pole-positioning is usually seen as an ancient superstition that what an animal sees during conception is somehow impressed upon the offspring. The notes in the *New Oxford Annotated Bible* (third edition), written by the Bible scholar David M. Carr, put it like this:

> *Ancient breeders believed that the female, at the time of conception, was influenced by visual impressions that affect the color of the offspring. Jacob produced striped animals by putting striped sticks before the females' eyes while they were breeding.*

A standard commentary on Genesis describes it as "prenatal conditioning of the flock by means of visual aids—in conformance with universal folk beliefs."[6]

In other words, people back then believed that if a dog wandered by while a couple was rocking and rolling and one of them, especially the woman, saw the dog, their child would have a face resembling that of a dog. We probably all know people to whom this has happened. According to this interpretation, therefore, Jacob was using an early form of genetic engineering.

But this interpretation poses an obvious problem for modern readers. We know that Jacob's tactics are unscientific and don't actually work. Jacob himself seems to admit as much later on when he tells Laban,

> These twenty years I have been in your house; I served you fourteen years for your two daughters, and six years for your flock, and you have changed my wages ten times. If the God of my father, the God of Abraham and the Fear of Isaac, had not been on my side, surely now you would have sent me away empty-handed.[7]

But this raises a theological problem: Why would God reward Jacob for trickery and deceit? Or is there another explanation?

Animal Husbandry

A recent article provides a way out of this quandary with a new and highly sophisticated interpretation involving fake sheep penises (finally!). The article is by Scott B. Noegel, a professor of biblical and ancient Near Eastern studies at the University of Washington, Seattle.[8]

Noegel notes some of the rather ho-hum problems with the usual interpretation. But then he scores a winner by pointing out that the earliest sources for the magical belief connecting what a woman sees during conception with the appearance of her child appeared only in the fifth century CE/AD and later, long after the story in Genesis had been written. What is more, says Noegel, the superstition related only to seeing living beings—humans or animals—but not to inanimate objects. This makes perfect sense. Otherwise, ancient shepherds would have believed that their animals might produce offspring that looked like rocks, trees, houses, or anything else in plain view when they mated. Finally, Noegel challenges the standard interpretation by asking why Jacob would try to get Laban's stronger animals to reproduce, as he does in verses 41–42, if the basic function of the rods was to act as aphrodisiacs. It doesn't make sense, given Jacob's motive.

Noegel's innovative proposal is based on a new understanding of the Hebrew phrase *el hammaqlot*.[9] This phrase is usually translated "at the sight of the rods" (or "in front of the rods"), to accord with the superstition and because of the statement in verse 41 that Jacob put the rods "before the eyes" of the flock. But the Hebrew expression in verse 41 lacks any reference to seeing or eyes. What, then, does *el hammaqlot* mean? Noegel takes *el hammaqlot* literally and translates it "upon the rods." These "rods," he posits, were a kind of *phallus fallax*—fake animal penises—demonstrating again why Noegel is the most well-respected ancient animal dildo scholar on the planet.

In support of this interpretation, Noegel argues that the ancient Hebrew readers would have immediately recognized the true nature of these "rods" in the story, not only from their shape but also because the word used for "rod" has sexual overtones elsewhere in the Bible. For example, the prophet Hosea used the metaphor of adultery to describe Israel's worship of other gods.

My people consult a piece of wood,
and their divining rod gives them oracles.
For a spirit of whoredom has led them astray,
and they have played the whore, forsaking their God.[10]

Noegel's translation of the first line is more explicit: "[My people] consult its rod, its *phallus* directs them." Go, Noegel!

Sheep Rods

Here's what Noegel thinks might have happened in the Jacob story. He notes that sheep and goat breeders know when females are in heat because they (the female animals, not the breeders necessarily) rub their vulvas on trees or sticks. He suggests that Jacob used this same technique to increase his own flocks at Laban's expense. Rather than using the rods to influence the color pattern of the offspring, Noegel says, Jacob set the rods up in the watering troughs when the normal-colored female goats came to drink and mate. These were the goats Laban was going to keep. The goats rubbed their vulvas on the smooth rods, satisfying their sexual urges so they would not mate. But Jacob allowed the goats with markings to mate normally, thus increasing the number of goats he would take. Jacob even took it a step further and used the rods for the stronger animals in Laban's flock, so that they did not reproduce, but he allowed the weaker ones to reproduce normally. So Laban's flock grew weaker.

Noegel adds two further considerations in favor of his interpretation. The first has to do with the double reference to troughs (NRSV: "the troughs, that is, the watering places").[11] There are two separate Hebrew words here, and it seems unusual that the author would introduce two words for the same thing. The second word (*rahatim*) occurs only three other times in the Hebrew Bible, one of which is in this same story.[12] But another of its occurrences is in Song of Solomon, where it seems to refer to "tresses" of hair, possibly goats' hair.[13] Noegel suggests that in this story the word refers to the goats' hair that Jacob used to construct models of goat penises or even entire male goat mannequins as a further way of attracting the females in heat. Horny female goats just can't resist male goat mannequins.

Noegel also finds a series of similarities between Jacob's deception of Laban in this story and the way Laban tricked Jacob earlier into marrying Leah before Rachel. For example, we learned that Leah's name means "wild cow"; Rachel's name, Noegel notes, means "ewe." Also, Leah was said to have "weak eyes,"[14] but she was the one who bore more children, just as Jacob got Laban's weaker animals to reproduce. In addition, "Laban" means "white," which was the color of the peeled rods.[15] These and many other wordplays hint at a connection between the stories that tell us that Jacob paid back Laban using Laban's own style of trickery.

A Sheepish Evaluation

We hope we've gotten Noegel's ideas right, because this is an extremely complicated story, as he himself admits. To begin with, the word for "flocks" (*tson*) occurs often without any clear indication as to whose flocks are meant, Laban's or Jacob's. There are also four different terms for markings ("spotted," "speckled," "striped," "streaked"), plus the word "dark," and their precise meanings and differences are uncertain. There are also different words for different groups of animals—sheep, goats, and lambs, in addition to flocks—

and also separate words for male and female goats. All these different categories and designations make it hard to determine exactly what Jacob did to which animals.

But as much as we like the idea of fake sheep penises, Noegel's interpretation does not completely clear up the confusion in this story. At points in his paper, he even adds to the confusion by seeming to mix up whose flocks are whose. Also, there is no way to verify that his translation of *el hammaqlot* is correct. Overall, his theory is entertaining but doesn't have the support to tip the scales in its favor.

But Noegel's interpretation appeals to us for other reasons. His recognition of puns and similarities between the Leah-Rachel episode and this one is insightful. Whether Jacob was using magic or sheep-breeding techniques, he was still tricking Laban the way Laban had tricked him. What goes around comes around.

Noegel's theory also gains traction in providing an explanation for the theological problem of God blessing Jacob's trickery. Jacob succeeded in hoodwinking Laban, not because of God's blessing, but because of his expertise with sheep-breeding. His success was not the result of magic or some superstition about genetics. It was the result of techniques and knowledge that he gained, ironically, in the long service of Laban. We suspect that Noegel is on to something, even if it remains uncertain if—and how—fake sheep penises fit into the scheme.

15

Did King David Have Penis Envy?

E VEN DEVOUT ATHEISTS usually know something about the story of David and Goliath. But even avid Bible readers might not remember the story of David and the Foreskins.

King David is one of the towering figures in the Bible and in all of Western civilization. Born the youngest son of an out-of-the-way family, David went from lone shepherd boy to Israel's king, guided by his faith and piety. Of all Old Testament figures, David arguably gets more ink than anyone. His life includes the well-known stories of his affair with Bathsheba, his conflicts with King Saul, the Goliath episode, and the many psalms that bear his name.

So why would David have been involved in an incident with other men's penises? The answer, as always, is found deep inside the Good Book.

The Measure of a Man

David's victory over Goliath with a sling and a rock launched his career. But the newfound fame also caused him problems. Immediately after the battle, as the Israelite army marched home victorious, women from the towns and cities of Israel came out singing and dancing, accompanied by various musical instruments. It was the world's first all-girl band. They sang,

> Saul has killed his thousands
> And David his ten thousands.[1]

King Saul heard this and took the lyrics as an insult to his military prowess. How could they compare him with David, a kid and a nobody? By this time Saul was a seasoned warrior. But he recognized the threat from David, a startlingly popular up-and-comer. As Saul put it, "What more can he have but the kingdom?"[2] The writer of the First Book of Samuel adds in verse 19 that "Saul eyed David from that day on." Yikes.

Saul did more than eye David. He began plotting to kill him, and that's where the story of the penises comes in. We know you've been waiting for it. Saul learned that his daughter, Michal, whom the story presents as your typical frigid Jewish princess (see 2 Samuel 6), was in love with David. Like most fathers-in-law, Saul wanted to kill the man who would marry his daughter. But Saul went about it circumspectly. He thought, "Let me give her to him that she may be a snare for him and that the hand of the Philistines may be against him." In other words, "Maybe I can use this to get the Philistines to kill David." Then Saul would be rid of his enemy and his potential son-in-law all at once. It would be a good day for Dad.

So Saul turned on the charm offensive. He told his servants to tell David that he would be pleased to have him as a son-in-law. But, as with all marriages in ancient Israel, there was a price to pay. Marriages then were business deals, not love stories. Daughters were a valuable commodity for purchase. A king's daughter was especially valuable because she brought wealth and social standing. In fact, neither Saul nor David spoke about marrying Michal. The expression they both used was "becoming the king's son-in-law." That—not the girl—was the prize.

But David was poor. He had lots of heart, and now lots of fame, but no money. He couldn't afford a king's daughter. So Saul played it magnanimous. "No problem," he told David through his servants, which were the ancient form of text-messaging. "The king desires no marriage present except a hundred foreskins of the Philistines, that he may be avenged on the king's enemies."

This was like saying, "Sure, you can marry my daughter. But first scale this tall cliff backward using only your toenails." It was an invitation for David to commit suicide. But David was plucky. He accepted the challenge. Maybe Michal was a real babe—or, more likely, David really wanted to be the king's son-in-law.

David may also have realized that he was in a catch–22. If he failed against the Philistines, he would be dead (that was one catch). But if he succeeded, he would become a close member of Saul's family, inflaming Saul's jealousy and suspicion even more. In the end, one of these indeed came true.

David took up the challenge, but apparently none of the Philistines RSVP'd to his penis-trimming party invitation, so David opted for plan B.

David, Meet Yossarian

To understand plan B we bring Joseph Heller into the picture, author of the era-defining satirical novel *Catch–22*. It would be fun to discuss the finer details of that book here, but that's what English Lit 101 is for and we have other fish to fry. Let us draw your attention instead to another one of Heller's novels called *God Knows*, published in 1984. This book was a runaway international hit with obscure Bible scholars like us, while selling poorly in the general population. It even had a terrifically subversive sexual joke in the title itself: *God Knows* (get it?). This had Bible scholars like us howling in our cramped subterranean offices on little-known college campuses across America.

But we bring up Heller for a reason, and not just because he, like David, was a gifted literary Jew who had combat experience and multiple wives. Rather, *God Knows* retells David's life from David's modern-day perspective. Heller was not a biblical scholar, but his fictional account offers real interpretive possibilities for the David story, including the passage we're considering here. In Heller's story, Abner, the commander of Saul's army, tells David that to become Saul's son-in-law, the price will be one hundred Philistine foreskins, please. David begins to calculate how long it will take him to perform each circumcision, figuring he will need at least five other Israelite men to hold down each Philistine while he makes the unkindest cut. Abner interrupts him to explain that Saul actually wants him to bring back the entire penis. Duh, David. Saul wants the Philistines dead, not circumcised. This thrills David, as it will be much easier to kill the Philistines than perform the bris for a hundred unwilling converts.

Fast-forward in Heller's book to the scene where David and his men have accomplished the task and are returning to Saul's court. Heller envisions them to be transporting a cart filled with uncircumcised penises, like some macabre parody of a New York City hot dog vendor. (That'll make you think twice about your next lunch, won't it?) Just as the women had done after his victory over Goliath, they emerge from the Israelite villages along the way to greet them with songs and dancing. But in the first village the music and celebration are suddenly broken up by horrible shrieks and weeping as one of the women points to the basket of penises and wails, "Urgat the Philistine is dead!" The village goes into an uproar. Some people want to stone her, while other women rush to console her and some even join her in mourning. Apparently Urgat was a popular guy.

Things get worse in the next village, as many more women weep and mourn at the recognition of the notable Philistine's defunct member. They then move from grief to anger and attack David and his entourage. David orders his men to mix up the basket of Philistine frankfurters and cover the cart so that they can complete their journey and deliver their cargo to Saul.

Stranger Than Fiction?

The real surprise is that Heller's fiction may be fact. At least, Herbert B. Huffmon, a professor of Old Testament at Drew University in Madison, New Jersey, thinks so. Huffmon recently presented a paper at a professional meeting in which he suggests that the foreskins in this story are a euphemism for the whole enchilada—that is, the entire penis.[3]

But we don't need Huffmon to tell us that since the dawn of history, victorious warriors have always brought home the enemy's body parts as trophies of war. Think of cowboys and Indians. When Indians won, they scalped the cowboys. And when the cowboys won, they forced the Indians onto small plots of worthless land in Oklahoma, broke treaties at a whim, and forced the Indians to integrate into white European society. Maybe it would have been better if the cowboys had just cut off their penises.

In any case, Native Americans did not invent scalping or body-part trophyism—it goes back to at least the fifth century BCE; the Greek historian Herodotus (Book IV) says the Scythians did it. Other cultures paraded around the hands, feet, and heads of their enemies. But Huffmon also points to examples of penises being used as war trophies. Some ancient artwork depicts piles of penises (usually uncircumcised) as symbols of victory over enemies in battle. In the thirteenth century BCE, the unrepentant penis collector and Egyptian pharaoh Merneptah, son of Ramesses the Great (godfather of the modern condom), claims to have collected more than thirteen thousand penises of his enemies, especially Libyans, after defeating them in battle. He then had a huge weenie roast, we assume.

Declining Membership

Huffmon's idea that David cut off their entire penises works, except for one thing—shrinkage. Penises, as we learned earlier, have no bones. When severed (or when simply unmotivated), they wilt like lettuce in the noonday sun. From that perspective, they make poor trophies. What began as a cartful of stacked cucumbers in the morning would, by evening, look like a sad pile of dead slugs.

But the advantages of penis trophyism (as Huffmon and his crazed followers call it) really do outweigh the shrinkage problem. Cutting off a man's penis, be he alive or dead, shamed him and his people (don't you think?). A penis-less corpse lying on the battlefield signified complete defeat. And a live man whose penis was cut off (à la John Wayne Bobbitt) would always occupy a lower status in society after that. (Mr. Bobbitt proved this by going on to make dirty movies with his reattached member.) In ancient cultures, penis-less men were considered not porn stars but, for all practical purposes, women.

Is it possible David cut off the Philistines' entire members, not just their foreskins? You bet. A recent scholarly article in the *Journal of Biblical Literature* took up this topic of wartime mutilation. (The *JBL* is the geek journal of the Society of Biblical Literature, the leading organization for academic study of the Bible in North America. People like us, who teach the Bible as a career, belong to it mainly because of their awesome holiday parties.) The article is by T. M. Lemos and is entitled, "Shame and Mutilation of Enemies in the Hebrew Bible."[4] Lemos looks at Bible stories involving mutilation of enemies. The Israelites were both victims and perpetrators of such mutilation. He concludes that mutilation was motivated by the desire to shame the enemy and graphically display power over them. Mutilation signaled a change in the status of the victims, moving them to the category of subjugated, defective, or lower-class persons. Lemos does not address David's circumcision of the Philistines, but his conclusion supports Huffmon's interpretation.

Now, to finish the story of David and the foreskins, the young hero met the requirement. In fact, the Hebrew text says he doubled it. He must have found where the Philistine men took a leak and ambushed them one by one as the Philistines waved sayonara to their favorite appendage. In the end David brought home two hundred "foreskins." Whether he brought a piece of each penis or the whole thing probably didn't matter much to the Philistines. One wonders whether David dumped the shrunken nubs on the palace floor before a stunned King Saul, who must have marveled at the Philistines' lack of endowment.

One more thing—why would the writer of this story have used the word "circumcision" as a euphemism? Perhaps because he knew he was writing the Bible and that sales would plummet in the Midwest if he said what actually happened. Or, more likely, the euphemism added a wry element to the story. The ancient writer and audience could well have understood what David really did. But describing it as circumcision instead of a complete amputation played on the fact that the Philistines did not practice circumcision (while the Israelites, Canaanites, and Egyptians did). The Philistines were known to Israelites as "the uncircumcised"—a lowdown dirty insult. By hacking off their manhood, David was, in effect, turning the Philistines into Israelites by circumcising them. The Israelites might have joked that this mutilation resulted in the Philistines' social improvement. Talk about sick humor.

16

Was Joseph a
Cross-Dresser?

I F YOU DON'T KNOW who Joseph from the Hebrew Bible is,
then you haven't paid attention to American theater for the past
thirty years. *Joseph and the Amazing Technicolor Dreamcoat,* a Broad-
way hit and a staple of cheesy high school productions ever since,
made this Bible character a household name. But to Bible readers,
Joseph was never obscure. Indeed, his story is the longest single narrative in the Hebrew Bible, taking up the final fifteen chapters of the
Book of Genesis. And it's as juicy as Bible stories come, involving
money, sex, power, and, as we are about to see, perhaps a hero who
dressed up like a girl.

The Clothes Make the Man . . . or Woman

Joseph was the second-youngest son of twelve brothers, and he was
Dad's favorite. His older brothers resented this, and one day when

Joey came out to visit them in the fields where they were pasturing the flock, they put Papa's pride and joy into an abandoned pit to let him die. If you've ever had family strife, be glad it didn't reach this level of treachery. (But if it did, please be sure to share this book with other guys in your cell block.) Then Joseph's brothers had second thoughts and pulled him out of the pit—so they could sell him to merchants who were passing through on their way to Egypt. The brothers then returned home to their father, Jacob, and told him that Joseph had been attacked and eaten by a wild beast. They provided irrefutable evidence: a bloody robe, the very robe Jacob had given Joseph to symbolize his favored status. The brothers had smeared it with animals' blood. Jacob believed he was experiencing every parent's worst nightmare and said, "It is my son's robe; a wild beast has devoured him. Joseph is without doubt torn to pieces."[1]

Joseph, meanwhile, was sold by the slave traders into the house of Potiphar, a powerful government official. He prospered there as a servant, but was eventually thrown into jail for a crime he didn't commit when he rebuffed the sexual advances of Potiphar's wife. After languishing in prison for a number of years, Joseph was suddenly set free when he was able to interpret the meanings of two troubling dreams the Egyptian Pharaoh had had. Joseph so impressed Pharaoh that he was appointed second in command over all of Egypt and successfully steered the country through the devastating famine that was the subject of Pharaoh's dreams. Joseph's life was one wild ride.

Zeroing in on the subject of the robe, which is the key to the transgender argument, we need first to discard the main myth people have in mind when approaching this story. As good as *Joseph and the Amazing Technicolor Dreamcoat* was for Andrew Lloyd Weber's pocketbook and PTAs everywhere, it has given many people a wrong sense of what Joseph's robe looked like. The coat is often presented as a wildly garish garment with colorful patterns stitched and woven into it. This is reinforced by the King James Version, an influential translation of the Bible that describes it as a "coat of many colors." Most people therefore imagine it as a cross between a bathrobe and the kind of Xtra-Large tie-dyed shirt you might spot on an aging hippie from half a mile away.

In fact, translations like the King James that highlight the coat's colors are based not on the original Hebrew text but on the Septuagint, the Greek translation of the Hebrew Bible. The meaning of the Hebrew text is less clear because the phrase that describes the coat (*ketonet passim*) is difficult to understand. The Hebrew term *ketonet* is well attested in the Bible as a type of garment, but the precise meaning of *passim* in conjunction with it is not as certain. The word usually refers to the palm of the hand or the sole of the foot, so it is generally believed that the phrase refers to a garment that reaches to a person's ankles and wrists. We might describe it as a full-length tunic. This is the basis of many recent translations like the NRSV, which calls Joseph's garment "a long robe with sleeves."

The uncertainty over how best to translate the Hebrew is compounded by the fact that the phrase *ketonet passim* appears in only one other place in the entire Hebrew Bible, and in that place it is worn by a woman. This is the story describing Amnon's rape of his half-sister Tamar, daughter of King David, where this type of garment is mentioned twice.[2] After the rape, the text offers an aside to the reader that provides some information about how Tamar was dressed. "Now she was wearing a long robe with sleeves (*ketonet passim*), for this is how the virgin daughters of the king were clothed in earlier times."[3]

The mention of the long robe with sleeves in only these two places—once to describe what the king's daughters wore and once in reference to Joseph's garb—has struck some observers as unusual. How can it be that the same article of clothing was worn by both males and females? Many commentators, including the early rabbis, have argued that it was probably an example of unisex clothing in the ancient world. According to this theory, a *ketonet passim* describes a type of garment that would have been worn by the children, both male and female, of important people.

Ready to Wear

But Theodore W. Jennings Jr., a professor at Chicago Theological Seminary, challenges that interpretation. Exercising good fashion sense, he believes the text in 2 Samuel 13 about Tamar leaves no doubt that the garment in question was something worn only by females.[4] In other words, Jacob had given Joseph a girl's outfit. Jennings, ever on the lookout for cross-dressing Bible characters, asks, "What are we to make of this curious case of transvestism?"

This jag into the subject of cross-dressing is part of a larger argument Jennings tries to make about the Joseph story as a whole. He maintains that the narrative presents the Bible's clearest example of transgendering. A transgendered person does not completely identify with or conform to the gender he or she has by birth. Transgendering can take a variety of different forms, including transvestism, the practice of wearing clothing associated with members of the opposite sex, à la J. Edgar Hoover.

Jennings sees Joseph as a transgendered character, and the robe his father gave him is the most visible outward manifestation of that. He goes on to argue that the narrative is actually the story of a young man in a family of males who were all struggling with issues of sexuality and difference. "Jacob/Israel has produced the queer Joseph, transvested him, and thereby transgendered him as a sign of his own masculine desire. And the progeny of Israel have engaged in the first instance of queer bashing," Jennings writes.[5] In other words, when Joseph's brothers sold him off to Egypt, they committed an anti-gay hate crime.

Jennings has company on some of his arguments. Commentators have frequently noted a pattern in Joseph's time in Egypt. On three successive occasions, Joseph encountered a more powerful man who was impressed by him and delegated some of his authority to him. The first was his master Potiphar, who put Joseph in charge of all the affairs of his house. When Joseph refused to have an affair with Potiphar's wife, he was sent to prison. There he met the chief jailer, who put Joseph over all the other prisoners. Finally there was Pharaoh, who, as mentioned, promoted Joseph to the number-two position in his government.

Jennings predictably sees a homoerotic element. He believes the repetition of this motif is a way of highlighting how attractive Joseph was to other men. He writes, "Thus, it seems that at every phase of his career, Joseph is carried upon a wave of masculine desire. The consequence of this desire is the designation of Joseph as a kind of surrogate for the male, almost as a kind of wife substitute."[6]

Jennings points to other parts of the Joseph story to support his transgendered reading. For example, he notes that the text calls attention to Joseph's good looks. He says Joseph's long robe with sleeves was not appropriate for working with the flock in the great outdoors, suggesting he was more at home in the home. He says that Joseph's rejection of Potiphar's wife suggests a lack of interest in women. He points out that when Pharaoh gave Joseph a wife, her father's name was identified as Potiphera, a not-so-subtle allusion to his former master. And finally, when Joseph brought his two sons to Jacob, the older man blessed them, thereby making himself, not Joseph, their father. Jennings even suggests that Joseph's success in prison may have been the result of sexual favors he performed for the chief jailer. If you're balking right now, we don't blame you.

Sizing Up the Proposal

Is Jennings off in some Elton John fantasy, or does his proposal have any merit? To start on the positive side, he rightly points out that Joseph's clothing seems to play a big part in the narrative. Note how many times clothing is mentioned. The robe with long sleeves indicated his father's preference for him, and it was later used to trick Jacob into thinking Joseph had been killed. When Joseph turned down the come-ons of his master's wife, he literally escaped from her clutches and left his garment in her grasp as he fled.[7] Before he left prison to meet Pharaoh and interpret his dreams, Joseph shaved and changed his clothes.[8] Finally, when Pharaoh promoted him to second in command, Joseph was dressed in fine linen clothes.[9]

Each of these references to Joseph's clothing signals a change in status for him, whether it be as the favorite son, the dead son, the prisoner-to-be, the former prisoner, or the Egyptian court official. Jennings's point that Joseph's robe is somehow tied to his status is valid.

Similarly, Jennings identifies some interesting connections between the Joseph story and the description of Tamar's rape in 2 Samuel 13 beyond the common mention of a *ketonet passim*. He notes that the beauty of both persons wearing the robe is mentioned, both wearers were assaulted by their brothers, and each time the robe became a symbol of violation and mourning.

But in our opinion Jennings has gone too far with his suggestion that the Joseph story is rife with sexual innuendo and can be read as the tale of a gay, transgendered young man. First of all, it's difficult to know exactly what to make of the long-sleeved robe. Because it is mentioned in only two places in the entire Bible, neither of which describes exactly what it is, we lack explicit information regarding its appearance and how it might have functioned in ancient Israelite society. Jennings believes it was a garment that was worn exclusively by females, but it's more likely that the alternative proposal is correct: that it was something worn by the offspring of prominent people. If so, Joseph's wearing of it early in the story could have been a way of prefiguring the high rank he would achieve later on when Pharaoh promoted him. This story includes several instances of foreshadowing like this. For example, Joseph's being thrown into prison recalls the scene a few chapters earlier when his brothers tossed him into the pit. This connection is even clearer in the Hebrew text, since the word for "prison" or "dungeon" (*bor*) is the same as that used for "pit."[10] It's therefore more likely that Joseph's robe is functioning as a marker of his future prosperity than as an indicator of his sexual identity.

Jennings's claim that the powerful men in Joseph's life all had the hots for him is also difficult to support. The story doesn't make a single reference to any such feelings on their part, and sometimes it supplies information that undercuts such an idea. For example, when Potiphar put Joseph in charge of his house, the text explicitly states that he did so because he saw that the Lord was with Joseph.[11] A couple of chapters later it says a similar thing about why Pharaoh promoted Joseph.[12] Jennings tries to get around this by arguing that the male desire originally was a central part of the story, but that it has been suppressed and rendered more subtle by the author's theological concerns. But that is just a naked attempt by Jennings to force the story to fit his preconceived interpretation. The story of Joseph is curious in many ways, but probably not for the reasons Jennings proposes. We may not know what made Joseph's robe so special, but you can file Jennings's ideas under "highly unlikely."

—∿—

17

Did Dinah Marry
Her Rapist?

MOST GIRLS DREAM of their wedding day from the time they are little, which is why, when weddings go wrong, it's so devastating for the bride. Grooms, who are usually more focused on the wedding night than the ceremony, typically don't care so much as long as there's a legal "I do" in there somewhere.

But an antsy-pants groom was precisely the problem in one of the worst wedding disasters in history, recounted for us in (where else?) the Bible's Book of Genesis, chapter 34, to be precise. In this account, a hot-to-trot neighbor boy fell for Jacob's only daughter, Dinah, and made his move without consulting Jacob or Dinah's twelve older brothers. Big mistake. These were some of the most overprotective boys in the Bible, and they had a twisted way of taking revenge.

A Sneak Attack

The story leaves much confusion as to whether the neighbor kid's offense was rape or just lack of cultural sensitivity. Here are the

details. Dinah, daughter of Jacob, was kidnapped (literally, "taken")
by a local Hivite prince named Shechem (whose name means "I
am clearing my throat"). Shechem had sex with her and then fell in
love with her—typical sequence for a guy. He then asked his daddy,
Hamor, if he could marry her. Daddy rolled his eyes and went to
speak with Jacob to settle what the young ones had done. Remember that in ancient times marriage was never primarily about love,
but about property, inheritance, and power. The bride and groom
were merely tools in the broader scheme of family and regional control. Hamor put the best spin he could on his boy's rush to the good
stuff and suggested that Jacob's family and Hamor's city-state could
intermarry and intermingle their land and livestock. Jacob was oddly
passive and seemed willing to go along with the arrangement. The
man who had wrestled with God was in no mood for a fight.

But Dinah's brothers were a different story. Young, reckless, and
ticked off in the way only big brothers can be, they gave Hamor a
deceitful answer. They said they were willing to grant the marriage
between Shechem and Dinah and to join peoples on one condition—that the Hivite men circumcise themselves. That surely was
a difficult sell for Shechem and Hamor to make to the other blokes.
Why get their tips trimmed just so Shechem could have Dinah, especially when there were plenty of nubile Hivite women around? But
the father and son convinced them that all the livestock and property of Jacob and his sons would become theirs—a big payoff for a
passing pain in the prick. So the boys in town went under the knife.
We can't help but wonder how this worked logistically. Did all the
guys line up with their drawers dropped like a high school athletic
team waiting for their physical?

In any case, Dinah's twelve brothers had a nasty trick up their
sleeves. While the Hivite men's newly unsheathed swords were heal-

ing up—or as the Bible puts it, "on the third day, when they were still in pain"—two of the brothers, Simeon and Levi, came around to settle a score.[1] The Hivite men, stumbling around cupping their codpieces, were unable to wield their swords literally or metaphorically. Simeon and Levi slaughtered all the men of the city. The other brothers did not participate directly in the massacre but were happy to plunder the victims, seizing all their property, including their wives and children.

Back home, Passive Jake heard the news and was horrified. He complained to Simeon and Levi that their actions would bring trouble to him from the other Canaanite peoples. But the boys replied that they could not allow Shechem to get away with treating their sister like a whore. With brothers like that, no wonder Dinah wasn't married yet.

Bed 'Em and Wed 'Em

Careful reading of this story raises a lot of questions, many of which are addressed in a literary way in Anita Diamant's Hebrew-chick-lit novel *The Red Tent*. Did Shechem actually rape Dinah? If so, why did he fall in love with her and want to marry her? Usually rapists view their victims as objects rather than long-term partners. If he was in love with her, why didn't he try to marry her through regular channels? Was he really that impulsive and/or horny?

What about Dinah? What were her feelings? Was she also in love with Shechem? And what about Jacob? Why so laid back? Didn't he care about his only daughter? Why would he even consider allowing her to marry a man who raped her, if that's what Shechem did?

We think there's more than the usual Genesis bizarreness going on here, which is why we were gratified to find a theory from Joseph

Fleishman, a Bible scholar who teaches at Bar-Ilan University in Tel-Aviv, Israel. Fleishman thinks the wedding disaster was due to a clash of cultures between the Canaanites and Jacob's family.[2] He argues that the Canaanites, among whom were included the Hivites, practiced "marriage by abduction." According to this custom, a groom did not ask the bride's father for consent beforehand, but rather kidnapped her with the intent of marriage and then consummated the marriage by having sex with her. (This is still quite common in Arkansas.) Any negotiations between the groom's family and the bride's family took place after the marriage was consummated. And such negotiations were conducted not for the purpose of changing the marriage but to establish a proper relationship between the two families, so as to decide who got the mules and the back forty.

Interpreting the story of Dinah in this light, Fleishman holds that Shechem did not rape Dinah. The verb "took," he says, has a dual function.[3] It means that he physically kidnapped her. But it also refers to marriage. Therefore, when he "lay with her," Shechem's purpose was not to rape her but to make her his wife. Shechem's looking a lot better in this light. The third verb in this verse, which states that he "humiliated" her (the NRSV translates the second and third verbs together as "he lay with her by force"), refers to Dinah's sense of shame at having been bedded before being wedded, which seriously damaged her reputation in the local True Love Waits Club. Shechem was truly in love with Dinah, and to soothe her feelings of humiliation he "spoke tenderly" to her (literally, "spoke to the heart").[4] He did not view her as a temporary sex object but as his future wife. This is also why Dinah stayed in Shechem's house after their sexual tryst.[5]

According to Fleishman, Shechem's actions were an acceptable way of marrying outside of one's own clan or tribe in Canaanite culture. That is why Shechem's father, Hamor, treated the situation matter-of-factly and went to negotiate with Jacob in a businesslike manner. The problem was that Jacob and his sons weren't real keen on marriage by abduction. Jacob's silence suggests that he felt he had no choice but to accept the marriage post facto, as long as the Hivites were willing to undergo circumcision. As a stranger living in the midst of Canaanite society, what else could he do? But his sons felt differently. They saw Shechem's treatment of their sister as a serious violation of their family's honor, and they took revenge like a riled-up bunch of McCoys.

Family Feud

Fleishman's interpretation gracefully answers the questions raised about this story. It accounts for Shechem's desire to marry Dinah after having sex with her. It also explains why Jacob may have been willing to allow the marriage. It even hints at what Dinah might have been feeling. These explanations make Fleishman's idea very attractive.

Furthermore, the idea of marriage by abduction has historical precedent, not least of which is the rich textual evidence found in *Seven Brides for Seven Brothers,* MGM's 1954 musical. The musical, loosely based on Stephen Vincent Benet's story "Sobbin' Women," tells of brothers who kidnapped women and took them back to their cabin in the Oregon mountains. If you like acrobatic dance and a lot of politically incorrect gender dialogue, this is your kind of movie.

But the sobbin' women story actually goes back further to another politically incorrect bunch, the ancient Greeks. Plutarch, the leading playwright of his day, wrote a story called "The Rape of the Sabine Women."[6] It tells how the legendary founder of Rome,

Romulus, got wives for the stinky, uncouth group of men who in-habited his city. Romulus proclaimed a celebration and invited many of Rome's neighbors, including the Sabines. As the celebration was about to begin, he signaled the young Roman men to come into the crowd and carry away women of their choice, kind of like spring break in Daytona Beach.

There are other stories of this nature from ancient Greece, includ-ing the well-known myth of Persephone's capture by Hades. There is even a story about marriage by abduction elsewhere in the Bible.[7]

But is there any evidence outside of this story that marriage by abduction was a custom in Canaanite society? Not really. The an-cient stories on which the idea of marriage by abduction are based, such as the one about the Sabine women and the one in Judges about the women at Shiloh, describe the practice as a last resort at a time of emergency. There is in fact no clear evidence of a regular practice like this in antiquity, including among the Canaanites. It is a conjecture on Fleishman's part. His interpretation is plausible, but by no means certain.

So, one has to ask whether Fleishman's theory is any more likely than the more traditional understanding of this story. The answer is, probably not. What happened in the story can be explained by hu-man nature alone. Shechem's rape of Dinah may have been a kind of ancient "date rape." When he got her alone (the story doesn't explain how), he went too far. But he still had feelings for her. Maybe she had feelings for him as well. So he kept her with him, plan-ning to marry her. Shechem got his father to negotiate with Jacob for Dinah's hand. It was not the usual custom, but Shechem was a spoiled prince and accustomed to having his way. Hamor was willing to offer great riches to Jacob to make his son happy. He also had de-signs on the property of Jacob and his sons. But Jacob's sons refused to be appeased and concocted a plan of revenge. The offense they took was only partly to do with the treatment of their sister. They saw Shechem's behavior also as a personal affront.

Fleishman's postulation of an unproven Canaanite custom isn't really necessary to explain any of this. This story probably doesn't depict a clash of cultures but rather a young couple's relationship that got off on the very wrong foot.

—◦◦◦—

18

Was Lot a Sexually
Abusive Father?

WE COME NOW to another Bible story that, were it made into a movie, would shock and repulse even today's jaded audiences. The main character, Lot, is one of those antiheroes. It's painful to watch as he makes one bad decision after another, his life literally crumbling around him.

One of the most repugnant scenes involves Lot's daughters and the disgraceful thing they did with their drunken father in a remote cave. But the question we take up here is, who did what to whom exactly? And what might Lot's story be telling us about the sordid desires of men who lived back then? Proceed with caution. This one gets ugly.

There Goes the Neighborhood

Lot was Abraham's nephew, which is perhaps the only reason he got any ink in the Good Book to begin with. The main part of his story pops up in Genesis 19, which tells of Lot's family's skin-of-their-teeth escape from wicked Sodom and Gomorrah. Those cities, as fundamentalists love to remind us, then took a flaming sulfur bath courtesy of God's heavenly spigot.

But back up a few hours to when Sodom and Gomorrah were your typical anything-goes kind of towns. In walked two visitors, but these were not your typical wandering wayfarers. They were angels on a mission from God, not unlike the Blues Brothers several millennia later. The angels had come from heaven to see firsthand just how depraved things had gotten in these towns, whose stinky reputations had caused an outcry in heaven itself.

Lot knew (that's a pun) the town well enough to know (there it is again) that the two strangers might as well have hung FRESH MEAT signs around their necks. After inviting the angels-in-disguise to his home, he "urged them strongly" not to spend the night in the town square.[1] The angels complied, and sure enough, the other men of the city began buzzing around Lot's house like flies on a dung heap, demanding that he bring out his visitors so they could rape (literally "know") them.

Ever the dutiful host, Lot begged his neighbors to back off and then offered them his daughters instead of his guests. Why he did this, we don't know. Perhaps he had skipped a few parenting classes. But it's possible that ancient readers would not have viewed this with the same horror as we do. They might have thought Lot was simply being a good host. In any case, the men of Sodom didn't want Lot's daughters. They wanted the new guys.

As it turned out, the angels didn't need Lot to protect them because, of course, they had angel powers. They struck the horny gang blind and urged Lot and his family to escape. When Lot dallied, perhaps grabbing the silverware and photo albums, they literally pushed him out of the city, telling him to flee. Lot, his wife, and his two daughters set course for a small town nearby named Zoar. Lot's sons-in-law stayed behind in Sodom, thinking that Lot was joking about heading for safety. When God rained down fire and brimstone, they perished. Then, as Lot and the women in his life were fleeing against this backdrop of smoke and flames, Lot's wife looked back at Sodom, against the orders of the angels, and turned into a pillar of salt. That's three down.

Now we come to the part of the story that is the focus of this chapter. Lot and his daughters became afraid to stay in Zoar and moved to the nearby hills, settling in a cave. His daughters apparently became convinced that there were no other men on earth who would have sex with them, so they decided to seduce their father and bear children by him. On successive nights, they got him drunk and had sex with him, first the older, then the younger. They each became pregnant and in time gave birth to sons they named Moab and Ben-ammi. The two boys were the ancestors of the peoples known as the Moabites and Ammonites.

Low-Down Dirty Insult

The somewhat sickening story of Lot is usually interpreted by scholars as a series of etiologies about the region around the Dead Sea. To refresh your memory, an etiology is a story that explains the origins of something—a name, a geological phenomenon, or a social custom, for example. The Lot story explains how the area went from being lush and fertile (according to Genesis 13:10–11) to being hot and barren—because God rained fire upon it. It also explains why the Dead Sea is lifeless and has a sulfurlike odor and mineral formations along the shore. The odor comes from the burning brimstone or sulfur that God rained down, and Lot's wife is a salt or mineral formation. Even the name Zoar is explained etiologically. "Zoar" means "small," and Lot calls it a small city.

The episode between Lot and his daughters is also often seen as an etiology and a rude jab at Moab and Ammon. These countries sat on the other side of the Dead Sea from Israel. (The present-day Jordanian capital, Amman, gets its name from ancient Ammon.) But the names Moab and Ammon are loaded with meaning. Moab looks and sounds like Hebrew *me ab,* which means "from father." Ammon is similar to Hebrew *amm,* meaning "people," and Ben-ammi means "son of my people." Both words can be seen as implying incest, and that's how the Israelite writer meant for them to be understood. It was the world's first "your mama" joke, if you will.

The story, then, was your typical knock on a despised rival. People do this today about neighboring states, countries, or even work colleagues. For instance, there's a joke going around our state of Tennessee that makes fun of Arkansas and Mississippi, both of which border it. The joke goes: Why did the Arkansan move from Tennessee to Mississippi? Answer: He wanted to raise the IQ of both states. We'll give you a moment to figure that one out.

Ammon, Moab, and Israel were neighboring states, so naturally, they made fun of each other. The point of the Lot story, as one biblical scholar put it, was to "prove" that the Moabites and Ammonites were descended from incestuous bastards. Take that.

When Is a Cave Just a Cave?

But the scholar J. Cheryl Exum (remember her from chapter 6?) departs from this standard view and takes the story down a very different road.[2] She wants to show that Lot's daughters weren't the perverts—Lot was, and most of the men of his era too. She starts by picking off the low-hanging fruit, pointing out that several features of the story don't make sense. For instance, if Lot was so drunk that he didn't know he was having sex with his daughters, how was he able to—how shall we put this?—rise to the occasion? And how did his daughters seem to know after just one experience with him that they were pregnant? (Neither of them had sex with their father again.) Scholars have long noticed these curious elements and have accounted for them by their etiological interpretation. That is, what's important in the story isn't all the details but the sordid explanation it offers for the Ammonites and Moabites.

But Exum digs deeper into the daughters' motivation and asks why they would hop on Pop if the town of Zoar, presumably home to at least a few men, was right around the corner. Did they really think no man would have them? Or were there no men nearby, and if so, why did Lot not discuss this problem with his daughters? Furthermore, if the human race was in danger of extinction, what did the daughters' two sons do for wives? How did they reproduce, and why were Lot's daughters not concerned about this matter? None of it passes the smell test for Exum.

Exum suggests that the story is told all wrong. Lot, she says, was an abusive father who committed incest with his daughters, smoothing the way with alcohol to act out his repressed fantasies of desire. As is typical in abuse cases, he blamed the victims, and so the story implicates the daughters instead of dirty old Dad. These are not Exum's original ideas, but her slant is slightly different from that of other feminist interpreters. Her method, as we saw in the "Abraham the Pimp" chapter, is to get the "narrator" of this story on the couch for some serious psychoanalysis. To understand this we offer this refresher course on how things work in ExumLand. By "narrator" she does not mean the author of the story, because such an author would have died long ago. Besides, she believes that the story as we have it was produced by one or more editors combining several sources. Rather, she uses "narrator" to mean "the cultural or collective androcentric unconscious" that gave rise to the story.

We should have warned you to brace yourself for some highfalutin academic-speak. "Androcentric," for those of you who have success-fully avoided studying Greek roots, means "focused on men." Exum treats Lot's story like a dream and psychoanalyzes it as a fantasy that operates with different meanings on different levels and betrays the subconscious not just of one man but of an entire male culture. As with Abraham earlier, she considers all of the characters in the story as "split-off parts of the narrator," representing the "fears, desires, wishes, and so on" that are parts of the "cultural male psyche." Her analysis is not designed to solve the problems presented by the story, such as the unusual features mentioned earlier, but to shed new light on them by showing how they operate on a subconscious level.

Through Exum's prism, Genesis 19 can be divided into three parts. The first part, where the angels save Lot, depicts the narrator's superego in full force. The superego always shows one's conscious control over situations, self, and others. In this case, the angels embodied the superego and inhibited the sexual fantasies manu-factured by Lot's id or libido. Exum then drags readers through a thicket of Freudian interpretation. She says that when Lot offered his daughters to the men of the city, it illustrated the narrator's con-trol over his daughters' sexuality. To allow himself to indulge in the fantasy of having sex with them, the narrator first imagined homo-sexual sex, which was even more abhorrent to him than incest. The blindness with which the angels struck the men was the narrator's "self-punishment" for his incestuous fantasy. Blindness symbolized castration, so the men groped unsuccessfully for the "opening," an allusion to intercourse with the daughters.

In the second part, the sons-in-law serve a similar function and also represent the superego. They stood in the way of the narrator's fantasy through Lot of an incestuous affair with the daughters. Therefore, they were quickly disposed of so that the fantasy could proceed. The same was true of Lot's wife, who was the final obstacle to the fantasy. Lot's reluctance to leave Sodom and his request to go to Zoar instead of the hills was another effort by the narrator's superego to prevent the exercise of the id's fantasy, which needed to take place in an isolated place where Lot was alone with his daughters.

In the third part, the narrator absolved himself of the fantasy by blaming the daughters and the alcohol. The repeated mentions of these matters (alcohol four times, sex with daughters five times) betray the narrator's enjoyment at replaying the scene. Despite his claims to innocence, the narrator proudly rounded out his fantasy by imagining his sexual potency in the daughters' birthing of two sons. Finally, Exum points out several terms used in the story that are sexually suggestive. Not the least of these is the word "cave," where the sexual fantasy is set. Exum echoes the suggestion of previous scholars that "cave" is a euphemism for vagina. How original.

Exum on the Couch

The problems Exum points out in the story have long been recognized by biblical scholars, and Exum doesn't imagine that her proposal resolves these problems. She only tries to explain why they are there and to give an intriguing alternative to the standard view. Fine. But the question is whether her interpretation improves on the more usual etiological one. We let Exum off the hook in chapter 6, but her treatment of the Lot story exposes the real weaknesses in her approach. First off, once you turn the story into a "dream," you put yourself into the realm of imagination where standard rules of biblical analysis go out the window. It's like falling down the rabbit hole with Alice. By entering into the narrator's fantasy life and insisting that therein lie the multileveled meanings and hidden desires, Exum clears the decks of any limits or controls on her own interpretations. The story suddenly means whatever she wishes.

Exum also plays fast and loose with Freudian theory, which, we should add, is outdated anyway according to our colleagues in the psychology department. For example, Freud posited the "Oedipus complex," according to which a man has a subconscious desire for an exclusive relationship with his mother. Freud thought the same could hold true for a daughter's desire for her father, and later psychologists entitled this the "Electra complex." But this is the opposite of what Exum believes takes place in the Lot story. She says Lot desired his daughters. She has flipped Freud's Electra complex on its head. To her credit, Exum admits her inconsistency and includes a rather lengthy disclaimer, but the bottom line is that she picks and chooses what she likes about Freud without remaining consistent or true to this approach. Perhaps she is right to do so, but her selectivity raises more red flags about her interpretation.

There is another, more disturbing aspect to Exum's reading, and if we weren't so secure in our manliness, we might take personal umbrage. By analyzing a collective unconscious, she seems to implicate all men, or at least all ancient Israelite men, as participants in this ghastly fantasy. Surely this is an unfair stereotype. The days of making blanket inferences about all people of another race, gender, or culture are long gone. But Exum thinks it's fair to speak of an entire male culture having sick, repressed desires. Perhaps the Freudian analysis should be turned on Exum, since her interpretation seems to reveal more about her biases than it does about the nature of the story or the storytellers, authors, and editors who produced it.

We're tired of tangling with Exum. Let's tackle something less Freudian and more straightforward and gross.

19

Did Ishmael Molest Isaac?

MANY PEOPLE TRY to follow the Bible's teachings so they can have a happy home. But the truth is, there aren't many happy homes depicted in the Bible. The real inheritors of the Bible example are families who have experienced divorce, deception, adultery, and incest or have a murderer or rapist in the family. The Good Book is simply loaded with bad kin. And it's a virtual handbook for how not to raise children. Most of us are better off doing as the Bible says, not as it shows.

In this chapter, we look at another ugly crime that may have to be added to the rap sheet of Bible family behavior: child abuse.

Brotherly Love

As we've seen before, brothers in the Bible express their love in funny ways. They murder each other, sell each other into slavery, and betray each other. One of the Bible's most detailed accounts of family discord centers on Ishmael and Isaac, Abraham's sons by different mothers. As some of you Bible-savvy readers may recall, Abraham remained childless for decades after God promised he would be the father of many offspring. Then Abraham's fortunes changed, and he had two children, one by Hagar, the Egyptian maidservant of his wife Sarah, and then one by Sarah herself. Again, that's two women, one man, and two children. And they weren't even living in Utah.

As anyone knows who has ever openly maintained sexual relations with his wife and the maid, this situation led to some catty encounters. Fortunately for Hagar, shotguns had not yet been invented. Sarah simply drove Hagar out of the family. In fact, Sarah did this twice, first when Hagar was pregnant with Ishmael. But that time Hagar returned and an uneasy truce was established. Seventeen years later, Hagar was again forced to leave the family, but this time the breach was much more severe and the reason for her leaving more ambiguous. The Bible says that Sarah witnessed some sort of encounter between Ishmael and her son Isaac. But what did she see? That question sets the stage for our next foray into highly distasteful interpretations.

Ishmael and Isaac were half-brothers, fourteen years apart in age. This means that at the time of this mysterious incident Ishmael was a full-blown adolescent and Isaac was just learning to pee outside the tent. Because this scene comes immediately after the mention of a banquet that Abraham threw in honor of Isaac's being weaned (and who hasn't enjoyed such wonderful weaning celebrations?), it's possible that Ishmael would have been about seventeen years of age and Isaac about three. To the best of our knowledge, the women had lived together in peace since Ishmael's birth. But whatever Sarah saw Ishmael do to Isaac was bad enough for her to toss out household stability and demand that Abraham banish Hagar and Ishmael forever.

So what exactly did Ishmael do? The Hebrew word used to describe his action is *metsaheq*, a form of the verb "to laugh."[1] (This is one of a series of puns in Genesis on the name "Isaac," which means "he laughs.") But "laughing" doesn't appear to fit the context, so most English translations of the verse render the word as "playing," and a few opt for "mocking," "scoffing," or "taunting." On first glance, it appears that Ishmael was making fun of his little brother. Ishmael's act was mischievous maybe, but not exactly unique or evil.

No Laughing Matter

But author Jonathan Kirsch perceives more sinister goings-on in this story.[2] Kirsch is an attorney and a journalist, meaning he has the distinct pleasure of belonging to two of the most despised professions in America. Perhaps to redeem his reputation, Kirsch has written several popular books on the Bible. But as the title of this one suggests, *The Harlot by the Side of the Road: Forbidden Tales of the Bible*, the book incorporates a healthy dose of sensationalism. According to Kirsch, Sarah's reaction is much too strong if what she saw was mocking. The punishment doesn't fit the crime. "We are asked to believe that, thanks to a single adolescent taunt by one sibling toward another, Sarah drives mother and son into the desert to die," he writes. We appreciate his skepticism, but we wonder if he's exaggerating things to increase his chances of getting on *Oprah*.

This issue is not new to biblical scholarship. This passage has puzzled commentators for centuries. Some early rabbis thought Ishmael was going beyond making fun and was trying to harm, or even kill, Isaac. For example, Rabbi Eleazar suggested that the two brothers went out to the field and Ishmael began to shoot arrows at

Isaac.[3] (Maybe Rabbi Eleazar had done this to his half-brother and was just projecting.) But nothing in the text supports this interpretation. As is often the case with early rabbis, this attempt to fill in a gap in the story has no basis. Sorry, gentlemen.

More intriguing is the proposal by the not so early (but never late) Rabbi Akiba. He says that Ishmael was fornicating with married women. How on earth did he get from "laughing" to "fornicating" (interested bachelors want to know)? He found the same verb *metsaheq* in the Joseph story, where Potiphar's wife used it to accuse Joseph of making a move on her.[4] The other place it's used, ironically, is with Isaac and Rebekah.[5] The pair was in Gerar, where Isaac attempted to pass off his wife Rebekah as his sister because he feared the local men would kill him if they knew they were married. The ruse was discovered when Abimelech, the king of Gerar, happened to glance out his window and see Isaac *metsaheq* Rebekah, which caused the king to realize that either they were in fact married or they had a very strange sibling relationship. Most English versions translate the word *metsaheq* here as "fondling." (Why was Isaac fondling his wife in public? Nobody knows, but we can just picture the servants leaning out the palace windows and shouting, "Hey, buddy! Get a room!")

In any case, given the clear sexual meaning of the verb on those other occasions, Rabbi Akiba claims that Sarah saw Ishmael seducing and making love to married women, thereby dishonoring them.[6] The problem with this theory is that Isaac is completely missing from it. But that's not all Rabbi Akiba's fault. In the version of the Hebrew Bible he was reading, the name "Isaac" is missing. For the rabbi, Genesis 21:9 reads, "But Sarah saw the son of Hagar the Egyptian, whom she had borne to Abraham, playing" (NRSV). Most English translations, including the NRSV, add *"with her son Isaac."* Why the difference?

Again, the answer goes back to *Star Trek,* or at least to *Star Trek*–sounding words. The Greek and Latin versions of the Bible are respectively called the Septuagint and the Vulgate, which we think would make great *Star Trek* villain names. Both the Septuagint and the Vulgate include the words "with her son Isaac." These translations of the Hebrew Bible are older than the manuscripts on which our Hebrew Bible is based. For that reason, many prominent scholars think the words "with her son Isaac" are original to the story.

So Rabbi Akiba didn't have the full story, but before dismissing him on a technicality, we must ask why the words "with her son Isaac" are missing from the Hebrew version. According to interpreters like Kirsch, the true nature of this passage was so disturbing that some readers preferred to erase it from the text. They did not want to deal with the possibility that this passage, in Kirsch's words, "records an incident of incestuous child molestation, a notion so shocking that it may have been literally written out of the Bible by the rabbinical censors."[7]

According to this view, the text originally described Sarah observing Ishmael *metsaheq* Isaac. This rather disturbing interpretation has some merit. It explains Sarah's strong reaction. It is supported by the use of the Hebrew word *metsaheq,* which can carry a sexual connotation. There is no way to know for sure if Ishmael molested Isaac, but it seems entirely possible, and it certainly fits the dismal pattern of Bible family behavior.

On the other hand, there are problems with Kirsch's theory. First, he overlooks the fact that *metsaheq* is a pun on Isaac's name. Some scholars suggest that what Sarah saw was Ishmael "Isaac-ing," that is, playing or laughing in such a way as to remind her that Ishmael, not Isaac, was Abraham's firstborn and therefore his potential heir. That's why she wanted Ishmael gone and why she told Abraham:

"Cast out this slave woman with her son; for the son of this slave woman shall not inherit along with my son Isaac."[8]

And why is the phrase "with her son Isaac" missing from the report of what Sarah saw? This may also be because of the pun. Not only does *metsaheq* sound a lot like "Isaac" in Hebrew, but the two words look alike too. This means that a scribe's eye could have accidentally skipped from *metsaheq* to "Isaac" and left out the phrase "with her son Isaac." (This type of mistake is called a haplography, another word you can use to entertain and impress party guests.)

This explanation of what Sarah saw isn't nearly as sensational as Kirsch's theory, but it has just as much chance of being right—maybe even more. Perhaps Kirsch's instincts as a lawyer and journalist led him to put forth a titillating interpretation when a more plausible one was close at hand. In this case, the weight of the evidence is against him.

20

Was Moses Suicidal?

MOSES EXPERIENCED a lot of strange stuff—God spoke to him from a burning bush that wasn't consumed by the flames, walls of water piled high around him at the Red Sea, and God himself appeared to him in a cloud of smoke, lightning, and thunder at Mount Sinai.

But perhaps the weirdest episode in Moses's life—and one of the weirdest passages in all of the Bible—involved a spooky night in the wilderness with his wife and newborn son.[1] This text has bedeviled Bible scholars for thousands of years. It's inscrutable. It's bizarre. And it's just the kind of thing we dig. We'll call this one "The Case of the Bloody Bridegroom and the Freaky Foreskin."

It Happened One Night

It started out like any normal day. The sun was shining. The birds that dared to live in the barren desert east of Egypt were singing. And Moses had just been commissioned by God to go to Pharaoh and demand that the Israelites be set free from their enslavement. Before heading to Egypt, Moses stopped by his father-in-law Jethro's place in Midian to pick up the wife and kids. They would camp all the way to Egypt, like a family on vacation. But between Jethro's house and Egypt, a macabre scene unfolded one night. The Bible tells us that while Moses and family were camped out on the side of the road (because the KOA was full), the Lord dropped by and tried to kill him. But Moses's wife, Zipporah, took a flint, cut off her son's foreskin, touched Moses's feet with it, and said, "Truly you are a bridegroom of blood to me!" So the Lord left him alone. Then Zippy added, "A bridegroom of blood by circumcision."

You are correct—it makes no sense. It sounds like a ghost story or a scene from a David Lynch film, and its Lynch-like ambiguity has made it notoriously difficult for scholars to interpret. The passage throws around "hims" and "hes" like someone is having a pronoun sale, but fails to say who the pronouns are referring to—meaning that we don't know exactly who is doing what to whom. We don't even understand the key action—whose feet are touched with the child's foreskin, Moses's or the infant's—because the original Hebrew text in verse 25 simply says "his." His *who*? we'd like to ask. The pandering translators of the NRSV and other English versions of the Bible (you know who you are) say flatly that Moses's feet were touched, but this is at best a guess, and a limp attempt to clarify things for the reader that are not actually so clear.

Also, as you know from past lessons in genital euphemisms, the word "feet" in the Bible sometimes refers to the genitals. If that's the case here—and the nature of the story points in that direction—then the weirdness factor of the scene goes even higher.

Commentators have typically explained this scene as an attempt by God to kill Moses that was thwarted when Zipporah performed an emergency circumcision on her young son and then rubbed the foreskin on some part of Moses's body. Even if that is what the text portrays, what on earth does it mean? Why did God want to kill Moses? How did God try to do it? What was the point of the circumcision? What was the deal with rubbing the foreskin on Moses? Who was the "bridegroom of blood," and what did that title mean?

Suicide, She Wrote

Into this morass of questions steps Pamela Tamarkin Reis, an insightful, self-taught scholar who didn't begin serious study of the Hebrew Bible until she was in her fifties. Without a Ph.D. or formal training, Reis has come up with many creative and plausible answers to textual questions that have never occurred to most traditionally trained scholars. Reis claims that her "state of ignorance" allows her to approach tough passages without preconceptions. And that strategy has worked for her: Reis has routed many other experts by having fifteen articles published in fifteen years in some of the most reputable journals in the field. Most of them are compiled in a book titled *Reading the Lines: A Fresh Look at the Hebrew Bible,* for those of you who like doing extra-credit work.

Reis takes up the "bridegroom of blood" passage in her own unique way, piecing together clues and evidence like a part-time Bible sleuth.[2] Her novel interpretation of the passage was sparked by a synagogue sermon. The rabbi that day mentioned that some early Jewish commentators suggested that Moses had divorced Zipporah to marry another woman, the Cushite wife mentioned elsewhere in the Bible.[3] This got Reis thinking about the possibility that Moses and Zipporah did not get along and that the emergency surgery Zipporah performed was done not to save Moses but to spite him. What if Zipporah, Reis asked herself, was not a heroine "but an enraged wife on a tear?" So began her investigation.

The Bible does describe Moses sending Zipporah back to her father Jethro, an act some scholars interpret as a divorce.[4] After looking at the possible reasons for such a breakup, Reis settled on the fact that Moses never acknowledged his true origin or divulged his identity as an Israelite. She thinks Zipporah may have been duped into marrying Moses because she thought he was the prominent upper-class Egyptian he appeared to be. When she discovered at their place of lodging that he was a runaway fugitive of slave ancestry, it was more than she could bear. She snapped and performed this spontaneous circumcision, which goes to show what some women will do if pushed too far.

With this as her working hypothesis, Reis then pondered some of the other mysteries the text contains. She got her next breakthrough at a used-book sale. While rummaging through moldering tomes, she opened one and read the sentence: "The father turned the business over to his daughter." The sentence "stuck with me like a tune one cannot get out of one's head," Reis wrote later. "In bed at night, I thought about it and mused over the fact that a foreigner could understand every word of it—'father,' 'turned,' 'business,' 'over,' 'daughter'—and still not know what the sentence meant."[5]

Cue the lightbulb over the head. Reis decided that the Moses story might contain idioms whose meanings are missed by modern readers. An idiom, just to remind you, is an expression like "kicked the bucket" or "down in the mouth" or even "you suck" whose meaning is not predictable just by examining the usual meanings of its constituent elements. In this case, the phrase "the Lord met him and tried to kill him" doesn't make sense to us.[6] As Reis points out, why does God have to "try" to kill Moses? Why not just zap him with a lightning bolt and get it over with? Also problematic is the reference to God leaving Moses alone, which doesn't appear to make much sense within the context of the story.[7]

Reis concludes that these two phrases are not meant to be taken literally because they are colloquialisms that would have had different meanings for their original audience. Just as you would never arrive at the meaning of "kick the bucket" by examining each word more closely, so the idioms in this passage can't be broken down grammatically. Instead, Reis suggests that the passage actually describes Moses's suicidal state as he wrestled with who he was and what he should do. According to Reis, the statement that God tried to kill him was an idiom meaning that God caused Moses to contemplate taking his own life, and God leaving him alone was another way of saying his self-destructive thoughts had passed.

Honey, We Need to Talk . . .

The cause of all Moses's angst, according to Reis, was that he was in the throes of an identity crisis. After all, he'd been scooped out of the river by Pharaoh's daughter, raised as a wealthy Egyptian, and later married into the family of Jethro, a prominent Midianite priest. But God was now ordering him to reconnect with his Hebrew roots by going to Pharaoh and demanding that he let the Israelites go free. Talk about a midlife career change.

In Reis's reconstruction of the events, Moses was partly responsible for the mess he found himself in because he had never come clean about his past. From the very beginning of their courtship, Moses did not dissuade Zipporah or her father from believing he was a prominent Egyptian. Even his last words to his father-in-law kept up the charade that he was a born-and-bred native of the land of the Nile. "Moses went back to his father-in-law Jethro and said to him, 'Please let me go back to my kindred in Egypt and see whether they are still living.'"[8]

But it all came to a head for Moses as he and Zippy prepared to bed down for the evening on their way to Egypt. He had been able to hoodwink Jethro and perpetuate the lie about his Egyptian ancestry, but Zipporah was bound to find out once they got to Egypt and met Moses's brother Aaron, who had been conscripted by God to help Moses convince Pharaoh to free their people. The thought of telling his wife that their entire relationship was built on a lie was too much for Moses to bear. The jig was up. His options had dwindled to only two. He could tell Zipporah the truth and suffer the consequences, or he could take his own life and avoid that unpleasant confrontation. Reis believes that the phrase "the Lord met him and tried to kill him" is a euphemism for the latter option.

Moses, of course, did not kill himself. He fessed up and faced the wrath of his wife. Reis thinks Zipporah was so enraged that she decided to mock the ritual most closely associated with Israelite religion—infant circumcision. She reached for the nearest sharp rock and cut off her infant son's foreskin as a way of saying, in Reis's words, "You are a Hebrew? Then why not perform the disgusting and barbarous rite of the Hebrews?"[9]

We know what you're thinking. Why would Moses's Israelite ancestry have come as a surprise to Zipporah? They were married after all—surely she must have noticed he was circumcised.

But Reis believes that wasn't the case because Moses was never circumcised. She thinks the practice had fallen into disuse during this time, and she cites several texts from the Book of Joshua to support her view. After Moses had died and just after their entry into the promised land, God told Joshua to "circumcise the Israelites a second time."[10] So many people participated in this mass ritual that the next verse tells us the place came to be called Gibeath-haaraloth, Hebrew for "the hill of foreskins."

This group circumcision had to be undertaken because the younger generation of men who had just entered the land were not circumcised during the period of wandering in the desert.[11] Reis argues that the same could be said about the men of the previous generation, including Moses, who were also never circumcised. The reference to the disgrace of Egypt being rolled away, which is an etiology to explain the origin of the place name Gilgal,[12] is for Reis a way of speaking about the failure of the Israelites to observe the circumcision commandment while they lived under Pharaoh's rule. Moses was therefore able to pass himself off as one of the Egyptians because when they were all in the locker room together, his body looked like theirs.

When his suicidal thoughts passed and he told Zipporah the truth, she cut off their son's foreskin and touched it to Moses's foreskin, or "feet," in order to, in Reis's words, "make a sign in blood on the flesh where there should have been a sign in the flesh."[13] Because the word for "bridegroom" in Hebrew is the same as the word for "son-in-law," Reis thinks the phrase that is usually rendered "a bridegroom of blood" is actually a mistranslation and should be read as "a son-in-law of blood." Zipporah was rebuking Moses, expressing her anger upon discovering his real identity and poking savage fun at the bloody, barbaric ritual of the Israelite community she had unwittingly married into. According to Reis, Zipporah's put-down ("I have you, a son-in-law of blood!") was her way of contrasting her unhappy marriage with those of her six sisters, whose marriages were in keeping with their father's high social status.[14]

A Woman's Wrath

These are provocative and interesting suggestions. But there are drawbacks and shortcomings to Reis's proposal, and she ends up raising as many questions as she answers.

First, as she notes, nowhere else in the Bible does it say that God tries to kill someone. In other words, the expression upon which her theory is built is extremely rare. Because there are no other texts to compare this passage to, she must look elsewhere for support. She says that the proposed idiom of God trying to kill someone reflects the ancient Near Eastern view that God could control one's mental state. She does a nice job trying to support her idea with material from later in Exodus, where God seems to play Pharaoh's thoughts and actions like a divine puppeteer. And the fact that this material also comes from the Moses story is indeed suggestive, but it isn't enough to substantiate Reis's interpretation, and other factors work against her reading.

One problem is the statement that God "met" Moses and tried to kill him.[15] Reis says the meeting is metaphorical, but in fact whenever the Hebrew verb *pagash* is found in the Bible it is never used in this way. There are ten occurrences of it, including this one, and each time it describes a physical meeting between people or, in a couple of cases, animals. The passage is therefore speaking of a physical confrontation, an encounter between God and Moses, and is not describing divine mind control at a distance, as Reis suggests. This interpretation is supported by the use of the very same verb only three verses later when God commands Aaron to "go into the wilderness to meet Moses."

A further problem is Reis's claim that Moses was not circumcised. In fact, the very Joshua material she cites challenges that idea. In Joshua 5:5, it says that all the Israelite men who left Egypt for the exodus were circumcised. Although the text does not mention him explicitly, this presumably included Moses. If he were in fact circumcised, it would be a blow to Reis's interpretation because Zipporah, and perhaps Jethro, would then have known about his origin. On the other hand, it is possible that the Egyptians themselves practiced circumcision during this period, an issue that is debated by scholars.

If so, then his circumcision would have been indicative of either an Israelite or Egyptian upbringing. Reis dismisses the latter option by claiming that Egyptians didn't practice circumcision at this time, but this is not necessarily true. The reason for Reis's insistence on the matter is obvious—her entire argument falls apart if circumcision is not a uniquely Israelite custom or if Moses is circumcised.

In addition to the problems just noted, Reis also bases her conclusions on inference and hypothetical reconstruction of what happened, like her claims that Zipporah didn't know Moses was an Israelite and that he was suffering from an identity crisis. These are plausible ideas, but they are not supported by the passage. In sleuthing, you aren't allowed to make up your own facts.

Reis generally does first-rate work and has offered creative solutions to other vexing textual problems. She also is living proof that you don't have to have an advanced degree to engage in serious critical study of the Bible. But she hasn't completely solved "The Case of the Bloody Bridegroom and the Freaky Foreskin." Ultimately, the text in this strange passage, full of gaps and ambiguities, complicates any effort to make sense of it. In all likelihood, we'll never know for sure exactly what happened on that dark and mysterious night when Moses and Zipporah pulled off the road and had this gruesome encounter.

21

Did Ruth and Boaz Have a Roll in the Hay at the Threshing Floor?

WE'VE ESTABLISHED that Jesus's ancestors were no saints. Jesus was called "the Lion of the tribe of Judah"—even though Judah slept with his daughter-in-law thinking she was a prostitute. King David is perhaps Jesus's most famous ancestor, and yet he did the nasty with another man's wife, then put the hit on him. What, pray tell, did it take to get dismissed from the messianic line?

Now we come to a scandal involving Jesus's great-great-great-great-great-great-great-great-grandmother, a charmer named Ruth. To understand Ruth, we must open a topic we find personally repellent: in-laws. Every normal person knows that his or her in-laws belong in psychiatric wards, prisons, or alien study projects. But some people, a very weird 5 percent of the population perhaps, actually like their in-laws. They want to be with them over the holidays. They want to hear their lame stories, dumb jokes, and offensive political views.

Ruth was one of these oddballs. Her own family must have been a complete bummer because she was willing, even eager, to leave them and live permanently with her mother-in-law. Here's how it happened.

A Happy Homecoming

Like any good story, this one began with a crisis—a famine that drove a particular Israelite family from their home in Bethlehem (as in "O Little Town of") to Moab on the other side of the Dead Sea (the modern country of Jordan). This family, led by the mother, Naomi, stayed there for ten years. Her sons married Moabite women, one named Ruth and the other named Orpah. For you daytime TV buffs, this is the very Orpah for whom Oprah Winfrey is named, though you'll notice that Winfrey's family mixed up the lettering by accident. It's probably better. Orpah Winfrey doesn't have that $1.2 billion net worth ring to it.

Speaking of unfortunate names, Naomi's sons were named Mahlon and Chilion, which in Hebrew mean "sickly" and "failing." Thanks, Mom. Soon the boys lived up to their names and died, leaving Ruth and Orpah as widows. Naomi's husband had died too. By the way, Naomi's name means "pleasant," and that would prove accurate eventually.

Having lost her husband and sons, Naomi decided to return to Bethlehem. Ruth and Orpah asked to join her, but Naomi convinced Orpah to go back home to Moab and become a daytime talk show host. Ruth, however, was undeterred. She pledged undying love and loyalty to Naomi.

Where you go, I will go; Where you lodge, I will lodge;
Your people shall be my people, and your God my God.[1]

These lines, which in King James English are "Whither thou goest, I will go," used to be sung a lot at weddings, usually by a soprano with a no-wonder-your-opera-career-never-got-off-the-ground voice. But Ruth originally directed these words to her mother-in-law. Keep that in mind the next time you hear it during the ceremony.

Why would Ruth insist on going with Naomi? All we can think is that she was hard up for options. Indeed, jobs for women were scarce in ancient Israel. Widows who had no male relative had three options: seeking charity, becoming a prostitute, or working for McDonald's, and unfortunately for them, the last option is a joke. Ruth didn't have a lot of choices, and apparently Sickly hadn't left her any life insurance.

So Naomi and Ruth went back to Bethlehem, where Ruth started a ground-level career in gleaning. Gleaning is picking up what harvesters drop or leave unpicked. Gleaning was Israel's welfare-to-work program for the poor. The law of Moses actually commanded farmers to leave a little of their crops unharvested:

> When you reap the harvest of your land, you shall not reap to the very edges of your field, or gather the gleanings of your harvest. You shall not strip your vineyard bare, or gather the fallen grapes of your vineyard; you shall leave them for the poor and the alien; I am the LORD your God.[2]

> When you reap the harvest of your land, you shall not reap to the very edges of your field, or gather the gleanings of your harvest; you shall leave them for the poor and for the alien: I am the LORD your God.[3]

In other words, God didn't want farmers to behave like Wal-Mart, but rather, to leave a little money on the table for the working poor. So Ruth began gleaning in the field of Boaz, who was a relative of

Naomi's dead husband. Boaz was impressed by Ruth's industry and by what he had heard of her loyalty to Naomi (who meanwhile had changed her name to Mara, which means "bitter," because she was mad at God). Boaz was very kind to Ruth, making sure she was not harassed by the fieldworkers and giving her water and food. He told his reapers to leave some of what they had picked for her. Boaz even asked her not to glean in another field, so Ruth gleaned in Boaz's field until the end of the barley and wheat harvests.

At the end of the harvest, Ruth had no more reason to hang around Boaz's fields, but Naomi recognized that a May-December relationship was developing. She went into matchmaking mode and told Ruth to bathe herself and put on scented olive oil, the ancient version of Chanel No. 5. Then Ruth was supposed to dress up and go to the threshing floor. This was the place where the barley or wheat was beaten to separate the inner kernel of grain from the outer chaff. The kernels were heavier and would fall to the ground while the chaff would be blown away. Naomi told Ruth to watch for Boaz, see where he lay down after eating and drinking, then go to him, uncover his feet, and lie down there.

Ruth followed these instructions. In the middle of the night, Boaz was startled awake and looked down to find his favorite gleaner lying at his feet. He asked who she was. Ruth told him and added, "Spread your cloak over your servant, for you are next-of-kin." "Spreading the cloak" was a metaphor for taking in marriage. Ruth was proposing to Boaz. He gratefully accepted and thanked her for pursuing him rather than a younger man.

But there was one fly in the ointment. By custom, if a man died childless, his brother was to marry the widow and father children in the name of the dead man. In the Book of Ruth, the custom had apparently broadened to include not just brothers but the closest male relative. But Boaz was not Ruth's closest male relative; another man was ahead in line for her hand. Thankfully for Boaz, that man couldn't marry Ruth without jeopardizing his own inheritance, so he passed up the opportunity. With that, Boaz married Ruth, and they had a son named Obed, who was King David's grandfather.

What Really Happened at the Threshing Floor?

Let's zero in on the action. Scholars have long puzzled over the exact sense of Naomi's instructions to Ruth and her execution of them at the threshing floor. Naomi's instructions were:

> Now wash and anoint yourself, and put on your best clothes and go down to the threshing floor; but do not make yourself known to the man until he has finished eating and drinking. When he lies down, observe the place where he lies; then, go and uncover his feet and lie down; and he will tell you what to do.[4]

Ruth obeyed, and this happened:

> When Boaz had eaten and drunk, and he was in a contented mood, he went to lie down at the end of the heap of grain. Then she came stealthily and uncovered his feet, and lay down.[5]

What was Ruth doing? Why did she uncover Boaz's feet? Some scholars have suggested she was waking him up by pulling the blankets off his feet and freezing his toes. But why go to all that trouble? Why not simply talk to Boaz during the day and say, "Hey, you heard what happened to Sickly. I'm available now, and you're looking pretty good"? Why do something as strange as crawling in bed with his feet and waking him up? Is this some kind of romantic chick thing, or are we misunderstanding the action?

You know well by now that the term "feet" in the Hebrew Bible can be a euphemism for the genitals. The Israelites must have known that the size of a man's feet correlates to the size of his boneless appendage. So perhaps when Ruth uncovered Boaz's "feet," she was really uncovering his private parts. But if so, it still doesn't fully explain what happened. In fact, it just raises more questions. Was she trying to make Boaz think they'd had sex so that he would feel obligated to marry her? This seems unlikely. Yes, Boaz was probably a little tipsy from "eating and drinking." That's what it means when it says that he was "in a contented mood" (literally, "his heart was good"). Harvest was a time of celebration, after all. But he wasn't like Lot—so drunk that he couldn't remember whether or not he'd had sex. (*That's* drunk.) Besides, he seemed very pleased that Ruth had come after him and doesn't seem to have felt coerced.

Who's Uncovered?

Enter Kirsten Nielsen, a Dutch Bible scholar who wants to save us from our confusion. In her commentary on Ruth, Nielsen proposes a new and unique solution to the quandary of this passage.[6] She begins by noting the sexual overtones of this episode. It takes place at a threshing floor, which is linked with celebration, as we have seen, and also with fertility rites, because nothing put ancient peoples in a squirrelly mood like a good harvest. Ruth waited until Boaz had eaten and drunk, which would have loosened him up sexually (and given him a good set of beer goggles, just in case). By bathing, perfuming, and dressing, she made herself irresistible to Boaz, Nielsen says. Nielsen also notes the obvious: the verb "to lie," a key word in the story, is often used in the Hebrew Bible as an idiom for sexual relations. Finally, as we have seen, the word "feet" is a common euphemism for the sexual organs, and the verb "uncover" is associated with an idiom for having sex.

Had she been at the top of her game, Nielsen might also have noted one other expression with sexual overtones. Naomi told Ruth not to make herself *known* to Boaz until after he had finished eating and drinking and then she was to *know* the exact place where he lay down and go to him there.[7] The verb "to know," of course, is the Bible's favorite wink-and-nudge term for sexual relations.

Nielsen also points out that the word for "feet" in this story is not the usual one in the Hebrew Bible. The word in Ruth is rare. It occurs in only one other place in the Hebrew Bible, where it is used in tandem with "arms" and clearly means "legs."[8] But this word for "feet" can also mean the place of the feet, as in "the foot of the bed." When Ruth lay down "at his feet" all night, it clearly means at the foot of where Boaz was sleeping, not next to his actual toes. But in verses 4 and 7, where Ruth uncovered "his feet," it is more ambiguous. Did Ruth uncover Boaz's actual feet, or did she clear a place around his legs? Nielsen and many scholars and translators think it refers to a place, not a body part. Fair enough.

Then Nielsen springs her original contribution on us. The key to understanding this passage lies in what precisely was uncovered, she says. The traditional interpretation says Ruth uncovered his feet. Some take this to mean she literally uncovered his feet, which makes no sense. Others think it means they had sexual intercourse. Indeed, the verb "to uncover" is part of an expression, "to uncover the nakedness of," that is especially common in Leviticus 18 as a eu-

phemism for having sex. But further consideration makes this less
likely because there is no reference anywhere in the Hebrew Bible to
a woman uncovering a man's nakedness. Whenever the expression
"uncover the nakedness of" is used, it means to "uncover" a female,
meaning to have sex with her. For example, Levitical law says, "You
shall not uncover the nakedness of your sister,"[9] and goes on to prohibit "uncovering the nakedness" of other close female relatives. But
when it talks about uncovering the nakedness of a *male* relative, it
means having sex with that man's wife. This is what the otherwise
confusing prohibition in Leviticus 18:7a means: "You shall not uncover the nakedness of your father, which is the nakedness of your
mother." Ruth's uncovering of Boaz's "feet" can't have the same
meaning as uncovering the nakedness of a man in Leviticus. There
is no biblical support for it. The closest parallels are the story of Lot
being tricked into sex by his daughters (see chapter 18) and the law
about a woman who grabs a man's genitals (see chapter 12).

So what did Ruth uncover? Nielsen thinks the answer is (ta-dah!)
Ruth herself. She proposes that what we witness in this story is Ruth's
"Hello, big boy" moment. This is not explicit in the text, but Nielsen
says the context and other texts in the Bible indicate that Ruth was
communicating her availability and showing Boaz the goods.

There is support for this in other Bible passages where a woman
uncovers herself. The prime one is Ezekiel's notorious depiction of
Jerusalem and Samaria as lewd whores:

> When she carried on her prostitution openly and exposed her naked-
> ness, I turned away from her in disgust, just as I had turned away from
> her sister.[10]

This and the other cases of women uncovering themselves are, ad-
mittedly, all described with disapproval, but Nielsen argues that the

whole point in telling the story of Ruth was to show how she was an extraordinary character who did extraordinary things and was rewarded for them. Incidentally, there are a few examples of men uncovering themselves. These include the infamous story of Noah's drunkenness[11] and David's dancing before the ark.[12] Noah's exposure was clearly unintentional, and David's case is ambiguous because he was wearing some clothing, though it was very flimsy.

Nielsen finds further support for her interpretation in parallels between the story of Ruth and that of Tamar in Genesis 38 (see chapter 8). Both women were widows for whom the prospect of re-marriage in the normal course of events was dim. Both were com-pelled to take matters into their own hands and to use trickery to get what they needed. Both used their sexuality to accomplish their goals. Tamar dressed as a prostitute. Ruth took off her clothes and gave Boaz a show. Her nakedness was (duh!) an invitation to Boaz to take her as a wife before she pranced around nude to other leading members of the Bethlehem community.

The Naked Truth: Evaluating the Proposal

Nielsen's proposal is intriguing and inventive. It clarifies an episode that is otherwise difficult to understand. If Ruth was trying to se-duce Boaz or even to allure him, it certainly made better sense for her to undress herself rather than him.

Unfortunately, and we say this with real regret, there is one big problem with Nielsen's proposal. The form of the verb "to un-cover" used in Ruth 3:4, 7 (piel) is transitive but not reflexive. For you non-English majors, this means that it must have an object. It must uncover something, and it cannot mean to uncover oneself or to undress. The latter meaning requires a reflexive form of the verb (either *niphal* or *hithpael*). Nielsen recognizes this, so she does not claim that the verb in Ruth can have a reflexive meaning—not exactly. Instead, she says that its object is "implicit." In other words, everybody knows Ruth uncovered something, but the text doesn't tell you what.

Sorry, gang. This is fudging. Nielsen's proposal is a semantic gimmick gussied up in a snazzy nightie.

But there is one possible escape hatch. Nielsen cites one other case where this same verb form has an implicit object and a reflexive meaning. She says,

> The verb "uncover" is used in Isa. 57:8 without a direct object, but with an implicit "your genitals.". . . The woman turns her back on Yahweh, uncovers herself, and makes the bed wide when she buys the love of the bed from her lovers.[13]

The problem is that the meaning of Isaiah 57:8 is not as clear as Nielsen implies. The NRSV has a footnote about the line using the verb "uncover"—"Meaning of Heb uncertain"—and the NRSV actually translates it with an object:

> For, in deserting me, you have uncovered your bed,
> you have gone up to it,
> you have made it wide.

"Bed" could even be translated as the object of all three verbs in these lines: "you have uncovered, raised up, and widened your bed." In any case, the fact that there is only one other place in the entire Hebrew Bible that has the meaning Nielsen wants to assign to the form of "uncover" in Ruth—and that this place is uncertain—seriously weakens her proposed interpretation. If the form of the verb in Ruth were reflexive, Nielsen's interpretation would make perfect sense. But scholars have long recognized that this is not the case, and that is the reason why no one else has proposed her theory.

We are left with the text in Ruth that states that Ruth uncovered Boaz's feet or legs or the foot of his "bed." Exactly why she did this and what happened at the threshing floor remain mysteries. But perhaps that is the point. With a story this loaded with romantic attraction and innuendo, maybe the author left it to readers to imagine exactly what happened under Boaz's covers.

22

Did Jacob Use Ancient Viagra®?

FOR MOST SINGLE GUYS, going from no sexual partners to four in the space of a week would be cause for celebration. But when it happened to Jacob the patriarch, he must have learned that the human body is not an unending font of sexual energy. Almost overnight his tent flap became a revolving door for spouses and concubines wanting to leave with more than they came with. We can only imagine that he longed for a night alone to recharge his batteries and just plain think. Poor Jake learned the hard way to "be careful what you wish for because you just might get it."

That's why it seems possible to us that Jacob had a little help in rising to the occasion night after night. Let's examine the hard facts to see if he might have relied on an ancient form of Viagra®.

Big Love

But first, just how did Jacob end up with four sexual partners? No, he didn't go hog wild with an Asian mail-order-wife scheme. Rather, as we know from chapter 14, he was tricked into marrying the "wild cow," Leah, when he was really in love with Leah's younger sister, "the ewe," Rachel. But we haven't yet mentioned that these two sisters brought other sexual partners into the relationship as well—their respective handmaids, Zilpah and Bilhah, who then became Jacob's concubines. To Jacob, it must have seemed like an embarrassment of riches (at least for the first couple of nights), especially since concubines were basically female sex slaves. In the world of the Bible, they were also sometimes called upon to act as surrogate mothers, usually when the wife was childless. But in this case, the concubines were pressed into service like overused backup incubators as Leah and Rachel competed in a high-stakes game of fertility, family status, and love.

Upon marrying Jacob, Leah and Rachel wasted no time in trying to build their dynasties through him.[1] This heated sexual competition lasted most of their adult lives. Leah took an early lead, giving birth to four sons in a row. The Bible says that because Leah was unloved, God opened her womb. Rachel, who was barren, complained about this to Jacob, who we assume was doing his best to impregnate his favorite wife, but her complaint only angered him. Who can blame him? By that time he was probably feeling as sore as an overworked mule, hobbling around the camp and longing for his bachelor days.

So Rachel did what any desperate woman of that era did: she made her husband sleep with her servant. What Jacob thought of this is unrecorded, but Bilhah bore two sons by him, and these kids were credited to Rachel's account. Leah, meanwhile, had stopped having children, but sensing a ninth-inning comeback by Rachel, she brought in her relief pitcher, the handmaid Zilpah, who bore two sons by Jacob. At that point, Jake the Stud had eight children. And here is where the plot thickens, because the births of his final five children involved a plant with very mysterious properties.

Harry Potter and the Bible

One day, Reuben, Jacob's oldest son, found some mandrakes in the field and brought them to his mother, Leah. Apparently this was a big deal, because Rachel found out about it and begged Leah to give her some. Leah refused at first, until Rachel promised that Leah could "borrow" Jacob for a night in exchange for the mandrakes. Jacob then slept with Leah and she bore her fifth and sixth sons, Issachar and Zebulun, as well as a daughter, Dinah. Rachel also bore two sons, Joseph and Benjamin.

What were these mystery plants, these mandrakes, and why did the Bible mention them? The story seems to imply that they played a role in the production of Jacob's last five children—in Leah's regaining fertility and in Rachel's overcoming barrenness. Fans of Harry Potter have a head start on this answer because in that series the young wizards-in-training are taught about the properties of mandrakes.[2] In Harry Potter's world, mandrakes restore people and animals that have been petrified, transfigured, or cursed to their original state. But mandrakes are also extremely dangerous. Their tops are pleasant enough—leafy and purplish green. But their roots are small babies whose cry is fatal to human beings.

J. K. Rowling's description is obviously exaggerated, but it's not pure fiction. Mandrakes are real plants. They have long been rumored to hold magical powers. And in fact, they do have narcotic properties and have been used at different times as an anesthetic to induce sleep and as a stimulant. The botanical name of mandrakes is *mandragora officinarum*. They are native to the eastern Mediterranean area, so they grow near Jerusalem and other parts of Palestine, especially in rocky places. They are a tuber or root vegetable, a species of the potato family, and as with potatoes and carrots, their underground root is their fruit. Their color is similar to the description in *Harry Potter*. They have dark green leaves around a purple flower, and their leafy tops grow close to the ground, like lettuce.

Here is where mandrakes get weird: the roots do often look like a small person, similar to what's described in *Harry Potter*. They are usually about the size of a little apple but have been reported to grow several feet in length. The humanlike shape and the narcotic properties of mandrake roots have given rise to superstitions and legends about them over the ages. In the first century CE, the Jewish historian Josephus reported that the mandrake plant would kill a person who pulled it up.[3] In the Middle Ages, a more colorful legend developed. Mandrakes were reputed to grow under gallows. They supposedly sprang from the semen or urine of the men who were hanged there and resembled them. When uprooted, they were thought to emit a horrible scream that would instantly kill any person or animal within earshot. Shakespeare alludes to this superstition in *Romeo and Juliet*, although in his version the effect of hearing the mandrake's scream is insanity rather than death.

> *Alack, alack, is it not like that I,*
> *So early waking, what with loathsome smells,*
> *And shrieks like mandrakes 'torn out of the earth*
> *That living mortals, hearing them, run mad.*[4]

J. K. Rowling obviously adapted these legends in writing her popular wizard books.

But the relevant legends for our story go back much further. Because mandrake roots sometimes looked like a tiny woman, they were thought to be able to make women fertile. They were also purported to be an aphrodisiac that could be used, as a prominent Bible dictionary delicately puts it, "to excite voluptuousness."[5] Think of them as the Spanish fly or green M&Ms of their day. There may actually be something to this legend, since their narcotic properties could lower a person's usual inhibitions.

Ancient languages confirm the connection between mandrakes and sex. The Hebrew word for mandrakes (*dudaim*) sounds like the word for love (*dod*). Some even suggest translating the word as "love-plants" or "love-apples." The name suggests that the ancient Israelites were well aware of the plant's properties. The name "love-apples" is especially appropriate in the one other place in the Bible where mandrakes are mentioned. In Song of Solomon, the woman summons her lover and promises to give him her love (*dod*) "when the mandrakes have given forth their fragrance."[6] It doesn't take a fan of erotic literature to understand that the image of mandrakes blossoming and opening their leaves or flowers to emit fragrance is probably a metaphor for female arousal. The Arabs too had a nickname for mandrakes—"Satan's apples" or "the devil's apples," a clear recognition that mandrake-eating could lead to wild times.

It's no wonder, then, that a tussle broke out between Leah and Rachel over the plant. Both women wanted to bear more children for Jacob. Both seem to have believed that mandrakes could enhance sexual arousal and performance. But whether the mandrakes actually worked is hard to say. Genesis credits God rather than the mandrakes for the additional births, explaining that God heard Leah's prayer and remembered Rachel and opened her womb. But from the point of view of the two competing sisters, it's abundantly clear that they believed they were using an ancient fertility drug.

And they may not have kept the mandrakes to themselves. While mandrakes are associated explicitly with female fertility and female sexual arousal in Genesis and Song of Solomon, it's not beyond the pale to imagine that Jacob needed some help as well. At this point in life, he had fathered eight children. His equipment must have been tired. He was probably older than both Leah and Rachel, about middle age, perhaps older. He was probably looking for any kind of stimulation he could get. Leah, whose appearance and charm had never done much for him in the bedroom, may have especially wanted to share her mandrakes with him. Leah had also stopped bearing children, suggesting that she may have reached menopause.

We cannot know for certain, but it seems quite possible that Jacob used the mandrakes as a kind of ancient Viagra®, and that the final four tribes of Israel were born with the help of the biblical ancestor of the little blue pill.

23

Were Samson and Delilah into S&M?

THREE THOUSAND YEARS before Fabio first graced the cover of a romance novel, there lived Samson, history's original tough-'n'-tender hero. Like Fabio, Samson was a long-haired, lusty strongman who could heat up a battlefield or a bedroom. And like Fabio, portrayals always show him locked in a steamy embrace with some exotic woman, the tragic lover caught in a passionate yet doomed romance.

But the similarities end there. While Fabio went meekly into half-stardom doing butter-substitute commercials, Samson lived in constant conflict with his enemies (and, as we'll see, his lovers), and his life ended with a bang. Every church and synagogue kid knows that Samson liked to inflict pain on his enemies. But one scholar prompts us to ask a strange question: did he also like to receive pain from his sexual partners?

Let's back up for those of you who snoozed through the Book of Judges in Sunday or Sabbath school. Samson was no ordinary guy. An angel foretold his birth and commanded his parents to raise him as a nazirite, which was a person who was separated or consecrated, as the

Hebrew-derived term implies. Nazirites dedicated their lives to God and had to follow three rules: (1) avoid grapes and all products made from grapes; (2) never cut their hair; and (3) never come in contact with corpses.[1] In Samson's particular case, though not in the case of all nazirites, not cutting his hair gave him superhuman strength.

But like many strongmen, Samson also had a strong weakness. He enjoyed too much the company of women, and the wrong women at that. The first woman in his life was his wife, an anonymous Philistine whom Samson married against his parents' wishes. We'll spare you the gory details, but this poor, nameless gal came to an unfortunate end when she and her father were burned to death by their fellow Philistines as a result of their association with Samson. Because of this, Samson went completely postal and killed one thousand Philistines with the jawbone of a donkey. (Didn't they have a two-week waiting period for those things?)[2]

The second woman mentioned in Samson's story was a prostitute he visited in Gaza. When the Philistines discovered that the Big Guy, who was their sworn enemy, was in their city having a tryst with one of their ladies of the night, the men plotted to ambush him as he left through the gate at the break of day. But Samson finished his business prematurely and left at midnight, not even bothering to have a smoke. On the way out he removed Gaza's city gates, posts and all, and carried them on his shoulders all the way to Hebron.[3] This qualified as his morning workout, and later he had a shake for lunch and a sensible dinner.

Your Lyin' Heart

This brings us to Delilah, the only woman in the narrative with a name, and the only one, we are told, whom Samson loved (cue the dramatic warning music). But let us clear up some misconceptions about dear Delilah that remain in the collective memory. She is most often thought of as a deceitful and conniving woman, a femme fatale who resorted to trickery to get what she wanted. But in actual fact, Delilah never tried to trick or hoodwink Samson, and she was marvelously upfront about what she wanted—to learn the source of his amazing power. Her initial request was blunt and unambiguous. "Please tell me what makes your strength so great, and how you could be bound, so that one could subdue you."[4] No feminine subtlety there.

At the same time, her motives were selfish because in seeking to hand over her lover to the lords of the Philistines, she hoped to receive the tidy sum of eleven hundred pieces of silver from each of them. Why would she do this? Well, why not? The Bible never says Delilah loved Samson. Her motive was apparently less about heart strings and more about purse strings. She was probably a Philistine herself, so she may also have been acting out of loyalty to her people. If she could turn a profit in the process, so much the better.

So three different times Delilah asked Samson to reveal the source of his strength, and each time he gave her a false answer. (Who was the deceiver, then?) First he told her that he could be bound by seven fresh bowstrings. When she did this, he snapped them like thread. Next he told her that using new ropes would do the trick, but he snapped those too. The third time he instructed her to braid his hair and make it tight with a pin. This reference to his hair implies that he was giving a now-you're-getting-warmer hint at the truth. But this didn't work either. He remained as strong as ever.

Finally, Delilah exploited his affection with a classic female strategy: "How can you say, 'I love you,' when your heart is not with me? You have mocked me three times now and have not told me what makes your strength so great."[5] This major-league pout worked (don't they always?), and Samson, fed up with her badgering, told her the truth. Then he dozed off in her lap. His head was promptly shaved and he was taken prisoner by the Philistines, never to escape. They gouged out his eyes and made him a slave and showpiece at their ancient World Wrestling Federation event.

Egads. Women.

The Games People Play

While forgiving Samson his poor relationship choices—after all, he didn't have access to eHarmony's twenty-nine-point personality test—we can still ask, is it possible to know anything more about this iconic biblical couple? Lori Rowlett, a professor at the University of Wisconsin, Eau Claire, thinks we can, and she offers an interpretation that will shock many Bible readers the way it shocked even us.[6] She believes the relationship between Samson and Delilah contains an element of kinkiness that can be read according to the rules and codes of sadomasochistic sex games. We're not real familiar with S/M terms and practices (and our wives very much appreciate that), but to understand this theory we dive ever so briefly into the strange world of leather and love.

S/M involves a partner who is dominant and one who is submissive. Rowlett says that Delilah can be seen as the dominant partner with Samson in the role of the submissive partner—or "butch bottom," to use her term. She points to the fact that Samson surrendered himself willingly to Delilah and allowed her to tie him up. Rowlett sees Delilah the Philistine as the exotic Other who dominated the Israelite Samson in a tale of bondage and humiliation that fit the pattern of sadomasochistic sex play. Even their banter can be interpreted this way, she says: "The constant give and take between the two lovers resembles S/M role-play, complete with ritual questions, hair fetishism and other power games."[7]

In Rowlett's analysis, Samson got bored with winning every time and became tired of Delilah's constant questions, so he engaged in an act of deeper submission by revealing his secret to her. This made him even more vulnerable and put her in a position of greater authority over him. In effect, she became the supreme dominatrix who now had complete power. The mighty hero who always dominated others was reduced to a submissive partner whose fate was no longer in his own hands. At the same time Delilah too was transformed from a deceiving temptress into a domineering mistress.

Wowsers. Are we still in Kansas?

A Painful Proposal

This is surely an interpretation of the Samson and Delilah story that few of us have encountered before. Before casting a critical eye on it, we should begin by pointing out that elsewhere in her article Rowlett makes some astute and important observations about the power dynamics present within the story itself and in the context out of which it emerged. She observes that the play between Samson and Delilah reflects the cat-and-mouse game God played with the Israelites throughout the Book of Judges, and it also underscores the political agenda of the author of the story. Reading the narrative from the perspective of S/M sexual games is a creative way of acknowledging and exploring these aspects of the text and its formation.

But that doesn't mean that the text describes Samson and Delilah actually engaging in S/M erotic play. As Rowlett states, the ultimate

purpose of S/M is to achieve bodily pleasure. Yet there is no indication in the story that this was the purpose or outcome of what
Samson and Delilah did. According to the story, Delilah's primary
motivation was money. Samson's motives were less clear, but we
are never told that his interaction with Delilah over the source of
his power gave him bodily pleasure. In fact, he was asleep when she
weaved his hair and bound him with various cords. Sleeping during
sex is, we think, a universal sign of disengagement.

And what about the fact that Delilah herself did not actually cut
Samson's hair but had a man come in to cut it for her? Rowlett simply
ignores this fact. She also does not explain why, each time he was bound,
Samson the Supposedly Submissive broke free and asserted his domi-
nance over Delilah. That doesn't fit the pattern Rowlett proposes.

Other questions pop up when we take into account the wider context and recurring patterns of Samson's story. A few chapters earlier,
when the Philistines persuaded Samson's wife to pry from him the
answer to a riddle he had posed, she, like Delilah, appealed to his
affection to get him to spill the beans. "You hate me, you do not really love me. You have asked a riddle of my people, but you have not
explained it to me."[8] Here, as with Delilah, Samson was worn down
by her constant pestering, so he eventually relented and told her the
answer to the riddle, which she passed on to the Philistines.

Another scene also anticipated what would happen later with
Delilah when Samson's fellow Judahites bound him with rope and
handed him over to the Philistines.[9] The rope melted like flax, and
he reached for the nearest jawbone of donkey and went on the kind
of Incredible Hulk–like rampage he was becoming famous for at the
Palestine Police Department.

Rowlett does not try to give an S/M spin to these earlier scenes,
nor should she, because there is no evidence to support it. But the

echoes with the Delilah story suggest that the author wanted the reader to understand and interpret the relationship between Samson and Delilah in light of what had happened earlier in his life. Imposing an S/M reading on the later scenes runs the risk of making them so unusual that the similarities with the earlier part of the story are missed or lost.

A final issue concerns the appropriateness of reading a story that is more than two thousand years old through the lens of S/M sex play. Sadomasochism is a relatively recent term that is partially named after Leopold von Sacher-Masoch, a late-nineteenth-century Austrian novelist who wrote extensively about the sexual pleasure he received when he was verbally or physically abused. It may strike some as misguided to apply such a modern concept to such an old story.

At the same time there is ample evidence that people in the biblical world engaged in all kinds of unusual and, in some cases, illegal activities in the pursuit of sexual gratification, including rape, incest, and bestiality. These still take place today, and it's not inconceivable that some people in the ancient world would have derived satisfaction from the experience of pain and submission. But is it part of the story of Samson and Delilah? We think not.

To be fair, Rowlett never comes right out and says that the text describes Samson and Delilah engaging in S/M sexual activity. Her intent is to explain what kind of interpretation of the story emerges when it is read from a sadomasochistic perspective. Such readings have become quite popular in some scholarly circles during the past couple of decades. The Bible has been put in conversation with unusual and atypical aspects of human experience, and the results have run the gamut from insightful to bizarre. It is, in a sense, a way of playing with the text, but it is not, in our opinion, a way that yields much about the Bible story itself.

So Samson's popular image remains intact, in our opinion. He was a strong guy whose lovers exploited his affection like an Achilles' heel. He made a career of killing the enemies of Israel—even killing thousands in his final suicidal act at a great arena—but we're far from convinced that he enjoyed pain and humiliation as part of his lovemaking. Like Fabio, he was probably a romantic at heart.

Conclusion

There you have it. We hope you've enjoyed our tour of bizarre and bawdy Bible interpretations. You probably didn't guess ahead of time that it would include forays into such topics as pimping, depression, and assorted sexual proclivities. And this was just the whirlwind seven-day tour. There are plenty more fascinating interpretations that we hope to explore in future books.

We've considered a wide range of proposals in this book. Some, like the suggestion that Joseph was a cross-dresser, are preposterous. Others, like the idea that Eve was created from Adam's penis bone or that the Bible commands pubic shaving, we found to be more reasonable, if still shocking. And who could ever forget the unsavory but plausible interpretation of Ehud using Eglon's toilet as an escape hatch? As weird and strange as some of these proposals have been, they give us a deeper appreciation of the variety of themes covered in the Bible. And who knows? Perhaps exposure to the seamy side of the Bible will inspire people to enter the field of Bible scholarship, seeing that they can explore sexy and outrageous topics like these.

We've seen that Bible passages can be interpreted in many different ways. Some scholars study language and word meanings, while others focus on archaeology and ancient cultural practices. They like to talk in fancy terms like "interpretive lens" about the approach they use to interpretation. Some of the lenses that have been used in this book are feminism, sociological analysis, and Freudian psychology. One of the reasons for the number and diversity of approaches to the Bible is that they are all dealing with people and events that are thousands of years old. It's not an easy task to describe what people felt and did and thought that long ago—which is why there are sometimes more theories than facts. But as this book shows, it is a task that can produce scintillating, provocative, and even convincing results.

The Bible consistently reminds us that religion, sex, and other sensitive issues often go hand in hand. This does not make the Bible any less the Good Book. It simply shows that the Good Book is also the Real Book. We trust that you've been entertained and informed and that you've been prodded to consider some old stories in new ways. We also hope that you'll keep thinking about them—indeed, some of them may prove hard to forget.

Notes

—⁓—

1. Which "Bone" Was Eve Made From?

1. 2 Samuel 16:13.
2. Exodus 25:12, 14; 37:3, 5.
3. Exodus 26:20, 26, 27, 35; 36:25, 31, 32.
4. Exodus 27:7; 30:4; 37:27; 38:7.
5. 1 Kings 6:5; Ezekiel 41:5, 10.
6. 1 Kings 6:15, 16.
7. 1 Kings 7:3.
8. Genesis 2:25.
9. Genesis 3:7.
10. See the section on rabbinic interpretations of this story in Kristen E. Kvam, Linda S. Schearing, and Valarie H. Ziegler, *Eve & Adam: Jewish, Christian, and Muslim Readings on Genesis and Gender* (Bloomington: Indiana University Press, 1999), 77–83.
11. Genesis 1:27; 5:2.
12. See Phyllis Trible, *God and the Rhetoric of Sexuality* (Philadelphia: Fortress, 1978), esp. 94–105.
13. Mieke Bal, "Sexuality, Sin, and Sorrow: The Emergence of the Female Character (A Reading of Genesis 1–3)," *Poetics Today* 6 (1985), esp. 26.
14. The following description of Zevit's proposal is based on a presentation he made at the 2004 meeting of the Catholic Biblical Association of America in Halifax, Nova Scotia, entitled "Tasking, the Aesthetics of Sin, and the Poetics of Punishment: Observations on the Hebrew Narrative of Genesis 2:4–4:1," and on an article by Scott F. Gilbert and Ziony Zevit, "Congenital Human Baculum Deficiency: The Generative Bone of Genesis 2:21–23," *American Journal of Medical Genetics* 101 (3): 284–85.
15. Genesis 2:23.
16. Genesis 29:14.

17. Genesis 17:11, 14, 23, 24, 25.
18. Ezekiel 44:7, 9.
19. Exodus 28:42.
20. Leviticus 15:2–3.
21. Ezekiel 16:26.
22. Ezekiel 23:20.

2. Does "Knowledge of Good and Evil" Mean Having Sex?

1. Genesis 2:16–17.
2. Genesis 2:9.
3. Or "like gods."
4. Genesis 3:4–5.
5. Genesis 3:1–7.
6. Jacob Milgrom, "Sex and Wisdom: What the Garden of Eden Story Is Saying," *Bible Review* 10 (6, December 1994): 21, 52, and "The Blood Taboo," *Bible Review* 13 (4, August 1997): 21, 46.
7. Deuteronomy 1:39.
8. Numbers 14:29.
9. 2 Samuel 19:35 (19:36 in the Hebrew Bible).
10. Genesis 3:20.
11. Milgrom, "Sex and Wisdom," 21.
12. Genesis 2:25.
13. Genesis 3:7.
14. Genesis 3:21.
15. Genesis 2:24.
16. Genesis 4:1.
17. Genesis 3:16.
18. *St. Augustine: The Literal Meaning of Genesis*, 2 vols., trans. John Hammond Taylor, Ancient Christian Writers series 41–42 (New York: Newman, 1982).
19. Genesis 3:5, 22.
20. Genesis 4:1.

3. What Was Eve's Curse?

1. Genesis 3:8–13.
2. Genesis 3:14–15.

3. Genesis 3:17–19.

4. Genesis 3:16.

5. See, for example, Phyllis Trible, *God and the Rhetoric of Sexuality* (Philadelphia: Fortress, 1978), esp. 126–28.

6. Adrien Janis Bledstein, "Was Eve Cursed?" *Bible Review* 9 (1, February 1993): 42–45.

7. Genesis 4:17.

8. Carl Sagan, *The Dragons of Eden: Speculations on the Evolution of Human Intelligence* (New York: Random House, 1977), 92.

9. Genesis 4:7.

4. Was Cain Clinically Depressed?

1. Genesis 4.

2. Mayer I. Gruber, "The Tragedy of Cain and Abel: A Case of Depression," *Jewish Quarterly Review* 79 (1978): 89–97.

3. Genesis 4:5.

4. Jonah 4:8–9.

5. Gruber, "The Tragedy of Cain and Abel," 94.

6. Genesis 4:6.

7. Genesis 4:7.

8. Genesis 4:8.

9. Gruber, "The Tragedy of Cain and Abel," 97.

10. Genesis 4:7.

11. Genesis 4:8.

5. Does the Bible Encourage Us to Drown Our Sorrows in Beer?

1. Ecclesiastes 1:1, 12.

2. Ecclesiastes 1:8.

3. Ecclesiastes 2:16.

4. Ecclesiastes 4:2–3.

5. Ecclesiastes 9:12.

6. Ecclesiastes 5:18; see also 2:24; 3:13; 8:15; 9:7; 10:19.

7. Ecclesiastes 11:1–2.

8. Michael M. Homan, "Beer Production by Throwing Bread into Water: A New Interpretation of Qoh. xi 1–2," *Vetus Testamentum* 52 (2002): 275–78.

9. Homan, "Beer Production," 275.

10. Proverbs 31:6.

6. Did Abraham Pimp Sarah?

1. See Genesis 12 and 20.
2. Genesis 26:7–11.
3. Genesis 12.
4. Genesis 20.
5. Genesis 26.
6. J. Cheryl Exum, "Who's Afraid of 'the Endangered Ancestress'?" in *The New Literary Criticism and the Hebrew Bible*, ed. J. Cheryl Exum and David J. A. Clines (Sheffield, U.K.: Sheffield Academic Press, 1993), 91–113.
7. Exum, "Who's Afraid," 97.
8. Exum, "Who's Afraid," 106.

7. Was the Toilet Ehud's Escape Hatch?

1. Judges 3:12–30.
2. Baruch Halpern, "The Assassination of Eglon: The First Locked-Room Murder Mystery," *Bible Review* (December 1988): 33–41, 44.
3. Judges 3:20.
4. Judges 3:20, 24.
5. Halpern, "The Assassination of Eglon," 40.
6. Judges 3: 24a.
7. Halpern, "The Assassination of Eglon," 41.

8. Was Onan a Jerk?

1. Genesis 38:8.
2. Genesis 38:9.
3. Genesis 38:11.
4. Genesis 38:26.
5. Thomas W. Laqueur, *Solitary Sex: A Cultural History of Masturbation* (New York: Zone Books, 2003).
6. See *New Catholic Dictionary*, definition available at: www.catholic-forum.com/saints/ncd06105.htm.
7. Deuteronomy 25:5–6.

8. Genesis 38:8.

9. Deuteronomy 25:7–10.

10. See 1 Chronicles 2:1–17; Matthew 1:1–17.

9. What Was Isaac Doing When Rebekah First Saw Him?

1. Gregory Vall, "What Was Isaac Doing in the Field (Genesis XXIV 63)?" *Vetus Testamentum* 44 (1994): 513–23.

2. Gary A. Rendsburg, *"LĀŚÛAḤ* in Genesis XXIV 63," *Vetus Testamentum* 45 (1995): 558–60.

3. Isaiah 5:25.

4. Proverbs 23:29.

5. 1 Kings 18:27.

10. Did God Hit Jacob Below the Belt?

1. Hosea 12:4 (12:5 in the Hebrew Bible).

2. S. H. Smith, "'Heel' and 'Thigh'": The Concept of Sexuality in the Jacob-Esau Narratives," *Vetus Testamentum* 40 (1990): 464–73.

3. S. Gevirtz, "Of Patriarchs and Puns: Joseph at the Fountain, Jacob at the Ford," *Hebrew Union College Annual* 46 (1975): 33–54.

4. Genesis 24:2.

5. Genesis 47:29–31.

6. Genesis 46:26.

7. Exodus 1:8.

8. Judges 8:30.

9. Isaiah 48:4.

10. Ezekiel 37:6, 8; Job 10:11.

11. Job 40:17.

12. b. Qidd. 25a.

13. Song of Solomon 5:4.

14. Isaiah 6:1–2.

15. Isaiah 7:20.

16. Exodus 3:5.

17. 1 Kings 12:10.

18. Song of Solomon 7:1–5.

19. Proverbs 25:12.

20. Genesis 25:24–26.

21. Jeremiah 13:22.

22. Hosea 12:3 (12:4 in the Hebrew Bible), adapted from RSV.

11. Did King David Have a Potty Mouth?

1. 1 Samuel 25.

2. 1 Samuel 25:3.

3. 1 Samuel 25:22, 34.

4. Peter J. Leithart, "David's Threat to Nabal: How a Little Vulgarity Got the Point Across," *Bible Review* 18, no. 5 (October 2002): 19–23, 59.

5. 1 Samuel 25:16.

6. 1 Samuel 25:37.

12. Does the Bible Command Bikini Waxing?

1. Leviticus 21:9.

2. Exodus 21:17.

3. Exodus 22:18.

4. Leviticus 18:23.

5. Leviticus 19:28.

6. Deuteronomy 25:11–12.

7. See Exodus 21:22–25; Leviticus 24:19–20.

8. Lyle Eslinger, "The Case of the Immodest Lady Wrestler in Deuteronomy 25:11–12," *Vetus Testamentum* 31 (1981): 269–81.

9. Jerome T. Walsh, " 'You Shall Cut Off Her . . . Palm'? A Reexamination of Deuteronomy 25:11–12," *Journal of Semitic Studies* 49, no. 1 (2004): 47–58.

10. 2 Kings 9:30–37.

11. 1 Samuel 25:29.

12. 2 Kings 19:24.

13. Genesis 32:22–32.

14. Genesis 46:26 and Exodus 1:5.

15. Song of Solomon 5:4–5.

16. Walsh, " 'You Shall Cut Off Her . . . Palm'?" 55.

17. Judges 1:6.

18. Jeremiah 9:25; 25:23; 49:32.

19. Walsh, " 'You Shall Cut Off Her . . . Palm'?" 56.

13. Was Jael a Dominatrix?

1. Judges 4–5.

2. Judges 4.

3. Judges 5.

4. Susan Niditch, "Eroticism and Death in the Tale of Jael," in *Gender and Difference in Ancient Israel*, ed. Peggy L. Day (Minneapolis: Fortress, 1989), 43–57.

5. Judges 4:21.

6. Ruth 3:7.

7. Jeremiah 4:30.

8. Judges 5:2.

14. Did Jacob Use Sex Toys?

1. Genesis 29:15.

2. Genesis 29:1–12.

3. Genesis 29:20.

4. Genesis 29:21.

5. Genesis 29:25.

6. E. A. Speiser, *Genesis* (Anchor Bible; Garden City, N.Y.: Doubleday, 1964), 238.

7. Genesis 31:41–42.

8. Scott B. Noegel, "Sex, Sticks, and the Trickster in Genesis 30:31–43," *Journal of the Ancient Near Eastern Society, Columbia University* 25 (1997): 7–17.

9. Genesis 30:39.

10. Hosea 4:12.

11. Genesis 30:38.

12. Genesis 30:41.

13. Song of Solomon 7:5.

14. Genesis 29:17.

15. Genesis 30:37.

15. Did King David Have Penis Envy?

1. 1 Samuel 18:6–7.
2. 1 Samuel 18:8.
3. The presentation was for the Biblical Colloquium meeting at St. Mary's Seminary in Baltimore, Maryland, October 29, 2005.
4. T. M. Lemos, "Shame and Mutilation of Enemies in the Hebrew Bible," *Journal of Biblical Literature* 125 (2006): 225–41.

16. Was Joseph a Cross-Dresser?

1. Genesis 37:33.
2. 2 Samuel 13:18–19.
3. 2 Samuel 13:18.
4. Theodore W. Jennings Jr., *Jacob's Wound: Homoerotic Narrative in the Literature of Ancient Israel* (New York: Continuum, 2005), 177–96.
5. Jennings, *Jacob's Wound*, 182.
6. Jennings, *Jacob's Wound*, 184.
7. Genesis 39:13.
8. Genesis 41:14.
9. Genesis 41:42.
10. Genesis 40:15; 41:14.
11. Genesis 39:3.
12. Genesis 41:38–40.

17. Did Dinah Marry Her Rapist?

1. Genesis 34:25.
2. Joseph Fleishman, "Why Did Simeon and Levi Rebuke Their Father in Genesis 34:31?" *Journal of Northwest Semitic Languages* 26 (2000): 101–16.
3. Genesis 34:2.
4. Genesis 34:3.
5. Genesis 34:26.
6. Plutarch, *Romulus*, 14.1–7. A version of the story is also recounted by the Roman historian Livy (1.9.6–11).
7. Judges 21.

18. Was Lot a Sexually Abusive Father?

1. Genesis 19:2–3.

2. J. Cheryl Exum, "Desire Distorted and Exhibited: Lot and His Daughters in Psychoanalysis, Painting, and Film," in '*A Wise and Discerning Mind': Essays in Honor of Burke O. Long*, ed. Saul Olyan and Robert Cully, Brown Judaic Studies 325 (Providence: Brown University, 2000), 83–97.

19. Did Ishmael Molest Isaac?

1. Genesis 21:9.

2. Jonathan Kirsch, *The Harlot by the Side of the Road: Forbidden Tales of the Bible* (New York: Ballantine Books, 1997), 49.

3. Jacob Neusner, *Genesis Rabbah: The Judaic Commentary to the Book of Genesis: A New American Translation* (Atlanta: Scholars Press, 1985), 253.

4. Genesis 49:17.

5. Genesis 26:1–11.

6. Neusner, *Genesis Rabbah*, 253.

7. Kirsch, *The Harlot by the Side of the Road*, 48.

8. Genesis 21:10.

20. Was Moses Suicidal?

1. Exodus 4:24–26.

2. Pamela Tamarkin Reis, *Reading the Lines: A Fresh Look at the Hebrew Bible* (Peabody, Mass.: Hendrikson, 2002), 93–103.

3. Numbers 12:1.

4. Exodus 18:2.

5. Reis, *Reading the Lines*, 95.

6. Exodus 4:24.

7. Exodus 4:26.

8. Exodus 4:18.

9. Reis, *Reading the Lines*, 99.

10. Joshua 5:2.

11. Joshua 5:4–7.

12. Joshua 5:9.

13. Reis, *Reading the Lines,* 100.
14. Exodus 4:25.
15. Exodus 4:24.

21. Did Ruth and Boaz Have a Roll in the Hay at the Threshing Floor?

1. Ruth 1:16.
2. Leviticus 19:9–10.
3. Leviticus 23:22.
4. Ruth 3:3–4.
5. Ruth 3:7.
6. Kirsten Nielsen, *Ruth: A Commentary* (Louisville, Ky.: Westminster/John Knox, Old Testament Library, 1997), 67–71.
7. Ruth 3:3.
8. Daniel 10:6.
9. Leviticus 18:9.
10. Ezekiel 23:18 (NIV).
11. Genesis 9:21.
12. 2 Samuel 6:20.
13. Nielsen, *Ruth,* 69.

22. Did Jacob Use Ancient Viagra®?

1. Genesis 29:31–30:24.
2. J. K. Rowling, *Harry Potter and the Chamber of Secrets* (New York: Arthur A. Levine, 1999), 92–93.
3. Josephus, *Jewish Wars,* VII, vi, 3.
4. *Romeo and Juliet,* act IV, scene 3.
5. *Smith's Bible Dictionary,* definition available at: http://www.ccel.org/ccel/smith_w/bibledict.html?term=Mandrakes.
6. Song of Solomon 7:13.

23. Were Samson and Delilah into S&M?

1. Numbers 6:2–6.
2. Judges 14–15.

3. Judges 16:1–3.

4. Judges 16:6.

5. Judges 16:15.

6. Lori Rowlett, "Violent Femmes and S/M: Queering Samson and Delilah," in *Queer Commentary and the Hebrew Bible*, ed. Ken Stone (Cleveland, Ohio: Pilgrim Press, 2001).

7. Rowlett, "Violent Femmes," 106.

8. Judges 14:16.

9. Judges 15:11–14.